Archaeology, Cultural Heritage Protection and Community Engagement in South Asia

Robin Coningham · Nick Lewer
Editors

Archaeology, Cultural Heritage Protection and Community Engagement in South Asia

palgrave
macmillan

Editors
Robin Coningham
Durham University
Durham, UK

Nick Lewer
Coral Associates Ltd
Skipton, UK

ISBN 978-981-13-6236-1   ISBN 978-981-13-6237-8   (eBook)
https://doi.org/10.1007/978-981-13-6237-8

Library of Congress Control Number: 2019933316

Cover illustration: © Melisa Hasan

This Palgrave Pivot imprint is published by the registered company Springer Nature Singapore Pte Ltd.
The registered company address is: 152 Beach Road, #21-01/04 Gateway East, Singapore 189721, Singapore

PREFACE

UNESCO and Durham University jointly established the UNESCO Chair on Archaeological Ethics and Practice in Cultural Heritage in 2014. The Chair team recognizes that cultural heritage and archaeology are drivers for creative economies and that their protection contributes to sustainable development. It recognizes that heritage can play a unifying role in post-conflict and post-disaster responses but also that unethical or unbalanced promotion may alienate communities, generate conflict and the destruction of heritage. Durham's UNESCO Chair addresses this challenge by shaping and contributing to debates on professional standards and responsibilities; legal and ethical codes and values; concepts of stewardship and custodianship; research ethics and illicit antiquities; and the social, ethical and economic impacts of the promotion of heritage, particularly at religious and pilgrimage sites. To enhance this programme, Durham's UNESCO Chair has worked with new partners and sponsors, to meet its mission to:

- develop new guidelines and exemplar material for postgraduate education;
- devise benchmarks for the measuring social, ethical and economic impacts of Cultural Heritage;
- provide capacity building to heritage professionals and managers in South Asia and the UK through workshops and on-site training;

- create opportunities for postgraduate research and education in the UK;
- and generate networks of heritage professionals, academics and stakeholders.

Community consultations offer the opportunity of exploring ways in which individuals and groups can be involved in the long-term sustainable protection of sites of archaeological and historical importance, to discuss the future sustainable development of tourism and pilgrimage to the site that benefits the local community, and to establish mechanisms for continuing community engagement in archaeological excavations, preservation and protection. This volume of case studies from across South Asia represents the UNESCO Chair's first collective steps towards these collective goals.

Durham, UK   Robin Coningham
Skipton, UK   Nick Lewer

CONTENTS

NOTES ON CONTRIBUTORS

Kosh Prasad Acharya joined the Government of Nepal's Department of Archaeology in 1978, serving as Head of Excavations Branch before holding the office of Director-General of Archaeology until 2009. Following retirement, he joined UNESCO as a Consultant and was appointed Executive Director of the Pashupati Area Development Trust until 2016, and is an Honorary Research Fellow attached to Durham's UNESCO Chair.

Lisa Choegyal is British-Born and has made Kathmandu her home since the mid-1970s. With a background in the private sector as a Director of Tiger Mountain, one of Asia's foremost adventure tourism pioneers, for the past 25 years, Choegyal has worked as a consultant in pro-poor sustainable tourism throughout the Asia-Pacific region.

Robin Coningham holds UNESCO's Chair in Archaeological Ethics and Practice in Cultural Heritage at Durham University and has extensive experience of archaeology and post-disaster heritage interventions across South Asia. He is interested in sustainable community engagement with archaeological excavations and site preservation, and the balance between heritage protection, pilgrimage and development.

Venerable Mahinda Deegalle is Professor of Religions, Philosophies and Ethics at Bath Spa University. He is the author of *Popularizing Buddhism* (2006) and editor of *Buddhism, Conflict and Violence in Modern Sri Lanka* (2006), *Dharma to the UK* (2008), *Vesak, Peace and*

Harmony (2015) and *Justice and Statecraft* (2017). His research interests are Buddhism, Politics, Ethics and Violence.

Zahra Hussain is an architect and cultural geographer based in Pakistan. Her research focuses on architecture and sustainable development particularly in the Mountain Communities of Northern Pakistan. She leads the Laajverd Visiting School Program that is invested in documenting, preserving and incorporating local architectural pattern language in contemporary mountain architecture.

Shahnaj Husne Jahan is Professor of Archaeology and the Director of the Center for Archaeological Studies at the University of Liberal Arts Bangladesh. She has been excavating the archaeological site of Bhitargarh in Bangladesh since 2008 and developed a blend of strategies to stimulate public interest in archaeological heritage preservation and management.

K. Krishnan is Dean of the Faculty of Arts and Professor of Archaeology in the Department of Archaeology and Ancient History at the Maharaja Sayajirao University of Baroda, Vadodara, India. His publications are in the field of ceramic petrology, archaeometallurgy, ethnoarchaeological studies, South Asian Prehistory and early historic urbanism.

Ram Bahadur Kunwar is Chief Archaeological Officer in the Government of Nepal's Department of Archaeology. Head of the Excavation Branch, he has led archaeological projects throughout Nepal, lectures on Nepali history, culture and archaeology and has published widely on these subjects. Mr. Kunwar represents the Government of Nepal in the Japanese-Funds-in-Trust for UNESCO project within the Greater Lumbini Area.

Anouk Lafortune-Bernard is a Ph.D. student affiliated to Durham University's UNESCO Chair in Archaeological Ethics and Practice in Cultural Heritage. Her research focuses on the social and economic impact of cultural heritage. She has done most of her research in South Asia, including sites in Nepal, Sri Lanka and India.

Nick Lewer was Professor of Peace and Conflict Studies at the School of Government and International Affairs, Durham University and is now Director of Coral Associates Ltd. He has worked widely in South Asia focusing on community engagement, dialogue processes, education and project monitoring and evaluation.

Vrushab Mahesh is Assistant Professor in the Department of Archaeology and Ancient History, the Maharaja Sayajirao University of Baroda. He was awarded a University Grants Commission Research Fellowship for his doctoral research and his research interests include art history, cultural heritage management epigraphy, numismatics and ethnographic and ethno-archaeological analysis.

Marielle Richon is an art historian, formerly Programme Specialist at UNESCO World Heritage Centre, member of ICOMOS and lecturer at IREST Paris 1 Sorbonne, Euro-Mediterranean University of Fes, Morocco and Aix Marseille University, France. Since 2013 she has been the Oriental Cultural Heritage Sites Protection Alliance's Project Leader for Nepal.

Rajendra Narsingh Suwal is Deputy Director of WWF Nepal and an animal ecologist specializing in ornithological studies, biodiversity conservation, ecotourism and community conservation. Mr. Suwal is an Ashoka Fellow, past member of Environment Protection Council chaired by Prime Minister of Nepal, and a member of UNESCO's International Scientific Committee for Lumbini.

Kai Weise is a Nepali national of Swiss origin and has a Master's Degree in Architecture from ETH Zurich. President of ICOMOS Nepal, he has worked on architecture, planning and heritage management throughout Asia. After the recent earthquakes in Nepal and Myanmar he has specialized in reconstruction and heritage protection in post-disaster contexts.

LIST OF FIGURES

LIST OF TABLES

CHAPTER 1

Introduction

Robin Coningham and Nick Lewer

Abstract Coningham and Lewer chart the interest of archaeologists and heritage management specialists in engaging with communities associated with sites of historical tangible and intangible cultural importance. Drawing from archaeological, social science, development and tourism literature, international charters and codes of practice, and discussions at the AHRC-GCRF sponsored Kathmandu Conference *Heritage at Risk 2017: Pathways to the Protection and Rehabilitation of Cultural Heritage in South Asia* in September 2017, the chapter notes participatory methodologies used in community consultation and then provides conceptual and operational issues, questions and themes which inform the backdrop to this book. The chapter next identifies context-specific and generic challenges for community engagement which are highlighted through the case studies in the book, which is the first of its kind to focus specifically on South Asia.

R. Coningham (✉)
Durham University, Durham, UK
e-mail: r.a.e.coningham@durham.ac.uk

N. Lewer
Coral Associates Ltd, North Yorkshire, UK
e-mail: nick.lewer@coralassociates.org

© The Author(s) 2019
R. Coningham and N. Lewer (eds.), *Archaeology, Cultural Heritage Protection and Community Engagement in South Asia*,
https://doi.org/10.1007/978-981-13-6237-8_1

1

Keywords South Asia · Community engagement · Archaeology

1.1   Introduction: Context

Home to one-third of the world's human population, South Asia has a corresponding richness of cultural heritage with 44 properties inscribed on UNESCO's World Heritage List and thousands of protected national properties. Although strikingly rich, South Asia's cultural heritage is a non-renewable resource and there have been a series of tragic, high profile events, which have irreversibly damaged that heritage.

Less visible within media reports is the equally concerning widespread grassroots destruction of South Asia's heritage monuments, cityscapes and landscapes caused by increasing pressure from agriculture intensification and resource extraction as well as the spread of modern urbanization, industrialization and investment in mega-infrastructure. The balance between heritage and development has been successfully reached at a number of sites but this is not always the case and there are many examples of irreversible damage. These range from the impact of the Orange Metro Line along Lahore's Grand Trunk Road in Pakistan and aspects of the reconstruction of Kathmandu's skyline after the 2015 Gorkha Earthquake (Coningham et al. 2018) to the recognition that over 50% of Buddhist sites in Pakistan's Charsadda District have been damaged by illegal digging as have two thirds of Buddhist archaeological sites in Anuradhapura District in Sri Lanka (Coningham and Young 2015: 96).

Motivated by this context, over 180 experts and professionals from a wide range of disciplines, including archaeology, conservation, architecture, heritage management, development, planning and economics from across South Asia and beyond along with local stakeholders, including community members, site managers, army, police and policymakers met in Kathmandu at the *Heritage at Risk 2017: Pathways to the Protection and Rehabilitation of Cultural Heritage in South Asia* between 4th and 7th September 2017 to discuss contemporary issues of the protection of heritage during natural disaster and conflicts, but also accelerated development. The event was sponsored by the UK's Arts and Humanities Research Council's Global Challenges Research Fund (AHRC-GCRF-AH/P005993/1), with support from UNESCO Kathmandu, ICOMOS (Nepal) and the Department of Archaeology (Government of Nepal).

Allowing interaction with, and feedback from, local stakeholders, community leaders, administrators and key disaster responders and first responders, the participants co-produced resolutions for the enhanced protection and rehabilitation of heritage following natural disasters, conflict and in the face of accelerated development in Kathmandu and the Greater Lumbini Area.

These resolutions stressed the collective agreement that community engagement should be an integral element of heritage interventions but that it should also be linked with realistic social and economic benefits to adjoining communities and to a clear strategy related to pilgrim and tourist activities. It also advocated the undertaking of regular monitoring and evaluation of protection and maintenance processes and the economic and social benefits that local residents receive from on-site activities. The delegates also recognized the need for additional targeted exchanges and training, with the adoption of training materials, to strengthen the capacity of national agencies and NGOs tasked with the protection of sites and monuments in the face of accelerated development. Finally, they recognized the urgent need for the development of a network of South Asian experts to formulate, share and implement responses to protect sites and monuments in the face of accelerated development and climate change.

In this context, community consultations offer the opportunity of exploring ways in which individuals and groups can be involved in the protection of sites of archaeological and historical importance, to discuss the future development of tourism and pilgrimage to the site that benefit the local community, and to establish mechanisms for continuing community engagement in archaeological excavations, preservation and protection. This volume of case studies from across South Asia (Fig. 1.1) represents our first collective steps towards these collective goals.

1.2   APPROACHES

There is a causal relationship between heritage, local people and their well-being. As a result of this bond, local communities and indigenous peoples are often committed custodians of World Heritage sites, where they play an important, and sometimes overlooked, role in the stewardship of the biocultural diversity of their environments. (Brown and Hay-Edie 2014: 5)

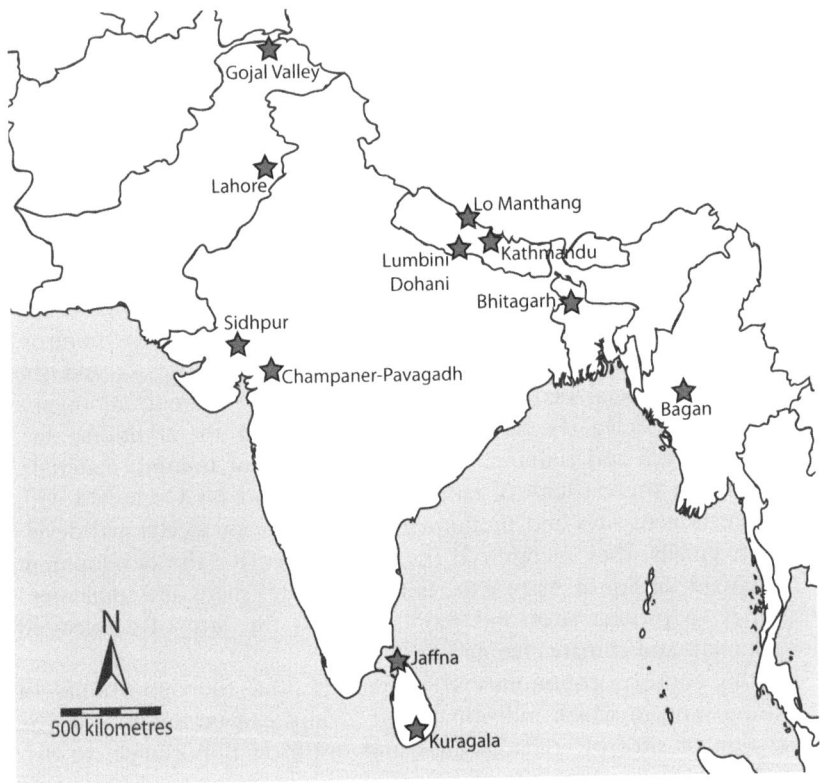

Fig. 1.1   Map showing the location of South Asian case studies

Community engagement in archaeological fieldwork and heritage protection has been of increasing interest to archaeologists and heritage managers. This is reflected in a literature that includes reports from conferences, a special issue of the *International Journal of Heritage Studies* (2010), Little and Shackel (2007), Smith and Waterton (2009), Sapu (2009), Waterton and Smith (2010), Silva and Chapagain (2013), Gould (2016, 2018), Brown and Hay-Edie (2014), Carman (2000), Moshenska and Dhanjal (2011), Perkin (2010), Schmidt (2017), Schmidt and Pikirayi (2016), Tully (2007), Watson and Waterton (2010), a number of International Charters and Codes of Practice including the *World Heritage Convention* (1972), the *Burra Charter* (1999), the *ICOMOS Nara Document on Authenticity* (1994) and *The*

Valletta Principles for the Safeguarding and Management of Historic Cities, Towns and Urban Areas (2011), and publications from the Getty Conservation Institute (2009), the Global Heritage Fund (2010) and UNESCO's World Heritage Centre (Albert et al. 2012).

Linked to this 'archaeological' interest is an established economic (tourism), conservation, development and social science literature containing broad-ranging debates about what the concepts of 'community' and 'participation' mean in theory and practice, including Oakley (1991), Burkey (1993), Chambers (1997) and Kothari et al. (2013) and this has been referred to by academics and practitioners in archaeology, heritage protection and tourism sectors (Winter 2009; Crooke 2010). Within this literature, it has been noted that communities are not usually homogenous or united but often characterized by tensions including issues associated with local power and business interests, group identity, access to resources, political influence, marginalization, religious differences and the impact of conflict or natural disaster. In the most positive sense, participation is envisaged as an approach that draws from, and values, local knowledge that can challenge top-down interests and development paths.

Methods used to engage communities include social surveys, opinion and perception polls, participatory and rapid rural appraisal (PRA/ RRA), participatory action research (PAR) and participatory learning analysis (PAL). In these methods, researchers and practitioners from outside the communities use a facilitative, empowering and listening discursive approach that enables them to learn from an engaged community. However, critics have pointed out that in some cases participation has been manipulative and may have reinforced Western concepts and approaches to inclusion. For example, research and analysis that is designed around a short term project can be defined more by agency needs and agendas rather than those of the people and community, that local culture and social relationships are not fully understood, and that if care is not taken dysfunctional local power disparities are maintained or even strengthened (Cooke and Kothari 2001).

There remains a challenge for archaeologists and heritage protection practitioners who want to engage (complex) communities in the excavation, understanding, interpretation, conservation and preservation of their cultural history. Methods and approaches that tackle such tensions in a meaningful and sustainable manner are still an issue and require a multidimensional and multidisciplinary team approach in which discipline interests and priorities need to be negotiated within the overarching context of 'what does a community think is best for them?' and 'how might we help them achieve this?'. The balance between site protection and community needs and interests can give rise to tensions. For example, when sites may be linked to community agricultural livelihood or religious practice, or when funding objectives and priorities do not mesh with community needs and perceptions of site importance, or when the local community has no connection with the culture of the site to be protected and sees it only as a resource.

1.3   Issues and Themes

We have identified the following conceptual and operational issues, questions and themes which inform the backdrop to this book.

1.3.1   Terminology

The terminology associated with this subject is wide, and definitions of community engagement vary depending on context. These include:

- Community engagement, community participation, community consultation, community custodianship;
- Cultural resource management, cultural heritage management, community-driven heritage engagement;
- Archaeological resource management;
- Archaeological heritage management, community heritage, heritage conservation, heritage protection;
- Public archaeology, community archaeology.

1.3.2   The Need to Engage Local Communities

In discussions relating to why is it necessary to engage local communities, a number of reasons have been identified and tried. These include:

- Educating and promoting understanding of what heritage protection is and why it is important, and the values and meanings of elements associated with it including historical, archaeological, scientific, economic, social, cultural, religious and political factors
- Explaining the importance of ownership and responsibility, to strengthen social capital and social fabric and increase capacity of stewardship of sites;

- Sharing archaeological skills and knowledge by outside experts with local people;
- Raising public awareness through outreach activities as to how local communities can participate in the preservation of sites by identifying risks and dangers and what they can do to protect or mitigate against these so that communities can become effective custodians or stewards of sites;
- Disseminating knowledge and information about the site, ongoing excavation programmes and research findings;
- Discussing methods and processes that will benefit the social and economic well-being of communities; this may be through local business enterprise schemes and links with the tourism industry.

1.3.3   Analysis and Understanding of Community Fabric

Underpinning community engagement and the design of partnerships with local communities is the need to understand social, economic, historical, political and cultural elements that inform both past and present contexts. To help with this process, systematic and sustained analytic methods should be used such as:

- Surveys and mapping to understand the social fabric and social capital in a local community associated with an archaeological site. This includes categorizing community identity groups and key stakeholders and analysing the relationships between them for connectors and dividers;
- Identifying outside stakeholders (regional, national and international) and mapping their relationships and interests in the archaeological site as well as assessing resources and capacities they might have;
- Constructing a framework of community engagement to ascertain who might be involved, and how, in the maintenance and protection of a site.

1.3.4   Community Engagement Activities

Archaeologists have acknowledged the importance of community engagement and have implemented activities and approaches that include:

- Raising awareness and interest in heritage protection through community meetings, talks by members of archaeology teams, and the production of information booklets;
- Involving people in excavations and field projects;
- Supporting festivals and cultural events;
- Promoting handicraft and local culture, including provision of small grants to assist local business opportunities;
- Suggesting and participating in education and vocational skill capacity building, forming archaeology clubs;
- Knowledge exchange between outside experts and local people;
- Tourism development and impact research.

1.4   CHALLENGES FOR COMMUNITY ENGAGEMENT

It is evident from the literature and prevailing practice that many challenges, context-specific and generic, still remain when designing community engagement strategies. These will be picked up by the case study authors throughout the book but include:

- Community Cohesion: for community-led initiatives to coalesce in terms of ownership, inclusiveness, trust building and power-sharing, flexibility and patience is needed to ensure the participation of local development and peacebuilding NGOs and CBOs.
- Inclusion: broad participation needs to be ensured so that civil society is strengthened as a counterbalance to local power structures which may be perceived as good or bad. In terms of setting up community engagement processes, important questions that need to be asked are: who is involved and how are they selected? what do they do and at what level are they involved—consultation, management, decision-making, protection, social mobilization?
- Level of Engagement: the difference between volunteers and paid workers in community engagement needs to be rational and explicit.
- Transparent Processes: inclusive public participation is a key to ensuring community engagement and the strengthening of civil society.
- Sustainability: community-led processes take time and require a long-term commitment of support; this might mean longer term financial assistance, longer term support from archaeology teams,

continuing education and skills development, and repeated community surveys. There is also a challenge in keeping a community interested in between excavations at sites where there is little to be seen and of no apparent benefit for local people.

- Monitoring, Evaluation and Impact Measuring Mechanisms: a challenge for community engagement initiatives is the funding of benchmarking, monitoring and evaluation processes, and for longer term impact assessment. The combination and linkage between social and economic data (qualitative and quantitative) requires interdisciplinary collaboration from the outset of a project.
- Political Interest and Corruption: there may be interference from political interests on site development and protection and this can affect the manner in which a community is prepared to become engaged. It is helpful to ascertain whether political interest is positive or negative and how close the relationship of local people to political parties might be and why this is.
- Role of Outside Activist Groups: may mobilize communities to oppose excavations and agitate for greater community involvement. This takes time and energy from archaeologists and technical experts.
- Conflict: contested ownership and claim to a heritage location between identity groups (such as religious) can lead to violence, political interference and problems for maintenance and protection. This impacts on how and why local communities become engaged.
- Destruction, Vandalism and Looting: 'theological' and cultural identity attacks on religious sites with or without support of a local community requires specific types of community engagement in protection measures. Local communities may be involved in looting.
- Conflict Prevention and Resolution: setting up new mechanisms or building on existing processes to resolve conflicts associated with the site development may challenge existing structures and cause problems. Approaches might combine traditional methods with 'newer' ideas.
- Impact of Tourism: communities may be worried with regard to increased visitor numbers and their social and cultural impact on traditions and beliefs and influence on younger people.
- Coherence and Integration: the integration of the different levels of governance (local, regional, national, international) is needed

to ensure that there is complementarity of action between archaeological site excavation and protection measures with the wider economic and development infrastructure plans. This means regular consultation between the local community, business and tourism sectors perhaps designing an integrated framework for these factors. Deciding on a lead agency, organization or individual for this is helpful.

- 'Experts' Taking Communities Seriously: the engagement of local community in conferences and feedback loops does not happen much at the formal level of symposia and 'higher' level consultations. A challenge is to find ways of bringing local people into these forums so that their voice is listened to so that they have input at more conceptual and academic level where programmes and projects are conceived, reported, and assessed.
- Authenticity and Value of Objects: what is a truthful and credible expression of value (Nara Document on Authenticity)? Developing a common understanding about objects and land that is of value or of no-value to people is important. For example, to an expert something may be interesting, to a villager it might be rubbish. How is this commodified? Who decides what to keep and what to discard and on whose value and ethical base is this decided?

1.5   Book Content

Chapter 2 is written by Shahnaj Husne Jahan, who explores Bangladesh's national cultural heritage and then takes Bhitargarh as a case study to present how micro-heritage tourism can become an effective tool to improve social benefits and participation for the protection and safeguarding of the cultural heritage of Bangladesh. Her chapter will illustrate strategies for community-based outreach programmes to promote sustainable tourism as well as to stimulate public interest in micro-heritage preservation and management for socio-economic development of the community. To achieve a balance between income-generation, sound management of heritage and community involvement in heritage tourism, the collaboration of all stakeholders is paramount.

In Chapter 3, K. Krishnan and Vrushab Mahesh focus on the design and development of the Bindu Sarovar Museum at Sidhpur in the Indian State of Gurarat. A *sristhal* or pious place, Sidhpur is considered one of the holiest Hindu sites to perform *shradha* or post-funerary rites for one's mother. In this context, a group of academics, religious practitioners, policy makers and community stakeholders came together to fashion a modern museum, which presents myth, legend and religious and ritual practices. Drawing from the site's deep intangible heritage traditions, this chapter will evaluate whether this development met its stated goals of satisfying the intellectual curiosity of visitors, develop their sense of the past and awareness of heritage of the region and, finally, providing opportunities to generate income for resident populations.

The Venerable Mahinda Degalle addresses religious and ethnic tensions in Chapter 4, relating to the preservation of archaeological heritage of Sri Lanka with a focus on Kuragala, which has become a contested sacred site between Buddhists and Muslims. It contains a Buddhist stupa and a rock shelter, with third Century BCE Buddhist inscriptions, and also a shrine with a mosque dedicated to a Persian Sufi mystic. The chapter will consider debates surrounding politicization of 'sacredness' of Kuragala site. For Buddhists, the visible Islamization of Kuragala has been become a political and co-existence related community issue.

Chapter 5, by Nick Lewer, Anouk Lafortune-Bernard, Robin Coningham, Kosh Prasad Acharya, and Ram Bahadur Kunwar, highlights the historical and modern importance of the Greater Lumbini Area in Nepal within the context of archaeological sites and excavations and the importance of living cultural heritage preservation and protection. Using Dohani as a micro-heritage case study, the approaches and methodologies used for community consultation and community engagement initiatives will be described and their effectiveness considered.

In Chapter 6, Marielle Richon reviews projects working with communities initiated by the Oriental Cultural Heritage Sites Protection Alliance. She provides an overview of projects at Lumbini, Kathmandu's Itum Baha Monastery and the Medieval walled city of Lo Manthang in Upper Mustang. The objectives of the Upper Mustang project are the preservation of its tangible and intangible cultural heritage. The Gorkha earthquakes in 2015 generated an awareness among the Lopa community and stakeholders about the need to undertake preservation rapidly in order to protect the local culture for future generations. This chapter will explore the manner in which the Alliance contributed in building harmony between all stakeholders.

In Chapter 7, Lisa Choegyal reflects that World Heritage Site management is a complex task and that heritage resource managers need to understand the principles of tourism. Firstly, it is necessary to understand your visitors, as well as your product and attraction. Secondly, it is important to see the resource through the eyes of the community. Community consultations have the objective of empowering people to participate in resource management, heritage protection and tourism. Choegyal asserts that it is important that communities receive benefits heritage conservation, and a sustainable partnership exists between resource managers, stakeholder communities and the tourism industry.

Zahra Hussain discusses the mapping of the cultural landscapes in northern Pakistan in Chapter 8. Focusing on intangible heritage, she argues that conflicts and disasters pose considerable risk to intangible cultural heritage which is not always visible and cannot be easily protected as it requires deep engagement and analysis. This chapter will discuss how the process of documenting cultural practices and pattern language was carried out in the northern Valleys of Pakistan. It will highlight participatory mapping methodologies used in the field and how communities were involved in the process of generating, producing, reflecting and exchanging knowledge.

Chapter 9, by Rajendra Narsingh Suwal, describes Nepal's success in natural heritage conservation stewardship moving from a protection regime to a community participatory and revenue-sharing mechanism. He shows how innovative community projects helped assist animal protection, anti-poaching activities, habitat management, forest restoration and livelihood activities. Involvement by members of a community in the planning and decision-making process was essential for the success of these initiatives. Suwal suggests that this approach to community engagement, to which WWF Nepal has contributed, may prove useful for conservation stewardship of archaeological and other heritage sites.

In Chapter 10, Kai Weise examines community engagement, archaeology and heritage protection in Bagan, Myanmar. The chapter charts the difficult process of nominating Bagan for World Heritage status and raises concerns about threats to the cultural heritage site. The link between the monuments, subsurface archaeology and the landscape and the human activity of farming is noted. Recently, the local community has been strengthened because of governance opportunities through the newly elected government. Communities are now taking a lead in discussing the future of Bagan and this chapter presents a case study of a community that has only recently been politically empowered and is still finding confidence in its engagement role.

Chapter 11, by Robin Coningham and Nick Lewer, examines two case studies, the Orange Metro Line in Lahore, Pakistan and Jaffna Fort in Sri Lanka. These examples describe some of the broader (political, economic, post-war) problematic and sensitive issues associated with heritage protection and archaeological excavations in economic development and post-war contexts.

Our final Chapter, Chapter 12, reviews and comments on the key issues and lessons learned, both generic- and context-specific, from the case studies and discusses challenges for community engagement when built in as an integral part of the archaeological project process.

We acknowledge the generosity of Durham University and Durham's UNESCO Chair in allowing Chapters 1, 5 and 12 to be made Open Access to reach and influence as wide an audience as possible. Finally, it should be noted that diacritical marks have been dispensed with following the convention of the Cambridge Encyclopedia of India, Pakistan, Bangladesh, Sri Lanka, Nepal, Bhutan and the Maldives.

References

Albert, M. T., Richon, N., Viñals, M. J., & Whitcomb, A. (Eds.). (2012). *Community Development Through World Heritage*. World Heritage Papers No. 31. Paris: UNESCO. http://whc.unesco.org/en/series/31.

Brown, J., & Hay-Edie, T. (2014). *Engaging Local Communities in Stewardship of World Heritage: A Methodology Based on the COMPACT Experience*. World Heritage Papers No. 40. Paris: UNESCO.

Burkey, B. (1993). *People First: A Guide to Self-Reliant Participatory Rural Development*. London: Zed Books.

Carman, J. (2000). Theorising a Realm of Practice? Introducing Archaeological Heritage Management as a Research Field. *International Journal of Heritage Studies, 6*(4), 303–308.

Chambers, R. (1997). *Whose Reality Counts? Putting the First Last*. London: Intermediate Technology Publications.

Coningham, R. A. E., Acharya, K. P., Davis, C. E., Weise, K., Kunwar, R. B., & Simpson, I. A. (2018). Look Down, Not Up: Protecting the Post-disaster Subsurface Heritage of the Kathmandu Valley's UNESCO World Heritage Site. In L. A. Bracken, H. Ruszczyk, & T. Robinson (Eds.), *Evolving Narratives of Hazard and Risk: The Gorkha Earthquake, Nepal, 2015* (pp. 159–181). London: Palgrave.

Coningham, R. A. E., & Young, R. L. (2015). *The Archaeology of South Asia: From the Indus to Asoka*. Cambridge: Cambridge University Press.

Cooke, B., & Kothari, U. (Eds.). (2001). *Participation: The New Tyranny?* London: Zed Books.

Crooke, E. (2010). The Politics of Community Heritage: Motivations, Authority and Control. *International Journal of Heritage Studies, 16*(1–2), 6–29.

Getty Conservation Institute. (2009). *Conserving Heritage In East Asian Cities: Planning For Continuity and Change.* Los Angeles: The Getty Conservation Institute. http://www.getty.edu/conservation/publications_resources/teaching/management.html.

Global Heritage Fund. (2010). *Saving Our Vanishing Heritage: Safeguarding Endangered Cultural Heritage Sites in the Developing World.* Palo Alto: Global Heritage Fund.

Gould, P. (2016). On the Case: Method in Public and Community Archaeology. *Public Archaeology, 15*(1), 5–22.

Gould, P. (2018, forthcoming). *Empowering Communities Through Archaeology and Heritage: The Role of Local Governance in Economic Development.* London: Bloomsbury.

Kothari, A., Camill, P., & Brown, J. (2013). Conservation as If People Also Mattered: Policy and Practice of Community-Based Conservation. *Journal of Conservation and Society, 11*(1), 1–15. http://www.conservationandsociety.org/article.asp?issn=0972-4923;year=2013;volume=11;issue=1;spage=1;epage=15;aulast=Kothari.

Little, B., & Shackel, P. (Eds.). (2007). *Archaeology as a Tool of Civic Engagement.* Lanham: AltaMira Press.

Moshenska, G., & Dhanjal, S. (Eds.). (2011). *Community Archaeology: Themes, Methods and Practices.* Oxford: Oxbow Books.

Oakley, P. (Ed.). (1991). *Projects with People: The Practice of Participation in Rural Development.* Geneva: International Labour Office.

Perkin, C. (2010). Beyond the Rhetoric: Negotiating the Politics and Realising the Potential of Community-Driven Heritage Engagement. *International Journal of Heritage Studies, 16*(1–2), 107–122.

Sapu, S. (2009). Community Participation in Heritage Conservation. In *Conserving Heritage in East Asian Cities: Planning For Continuity and Change.* Los Angeles: The Getty Conservation Institute. http://www.getty.edu/conservation/publications_resources/teaching/management.html.

Schmidt, P. (2017). *Community-Based Heritage in Africa: Unveiling Local Research and Development Initiatives.* London: Routledge.

Schmidt, P., & Pikirayi, I. (Eds.). (2016). *Community Archaeology and Heritage in Africa: Decolonizing Practice.* London: Routledge.

Silva, K., & Chapagain, N. (Eds.). (2013). *Asian Heritage Management: Concepts, Concerns and Prospects.* London: Taylor and Francis.

Smith, L., & Waterton, E. (2009). *Heritage, Communities, and Archaeology.* London: Duckworth.

Tully, G. (2007). Community Archaeology: General Methods and Standards of Practice. *Public Archaeology, 6*(3), 155–187.

Waterton, E., & Smith, L. (2010). The Recognition and Misrecognition of Community Heritage. *International Journal of Heritage Studies, 16*(1–2), 4–15.

Watson, S., & Waterton, E. (2010). Heritage and Community Engagement. *International Journal of Heritage Studies, 16*(1–2), 1–3.

Winter, T. (2009). Tourism and Development. In *Conserving Heritage in East Asian Cities: Planning For Continuity and Change*. Los Angeles: The Getty Conservation Institute. http://www.getty.edu/conservation/publications_resources/teaching/management.html.

CHAPTER 2

Communities and Micro-Heritage in Bhitargarh, Bangladesh: A Case Study

Shahnaj Husne Jahan

Abstract Jahan highlights strategies for community-based outreach programmes to promote sustainable tourism as well as to stimulate public interest in micro-heritage preservation and management for the socio-economic development of local communities using Bhitargarh as a case study. It also focuses on how micro-heritage provide a sense of identity to the local community; how they reflect and shape the social, religious, cultural, political and economic milieu of Bhitargarh in particular, and Bangladesh in general; how micro-heritage tourism can be more meaningful and responsible to society by appreciating culture and traditions, and in what ways micro-heritage tourism becomes an effective tool to improve social benefits and participation for protecting and safeguarding cultural heritage of Bangladesh.

Keywords Bhitargarh · Bangladesh · Heritage · Tourism · Community

S. H. Jahan (✉)
Center for Archaeological Studies, University of Liberal
Arts Bangladesh, Dhaka, Bangladesh

R. Coningham and N. Lewer (eds.), *Archaeology, Cultural Heritage Protection and Community Engagement in South Asia*, https://doi.org/10.1007/978-981-13-6237-8_2

2.1   Introduction: Context

Communities and cultural heritage are inseparable from one another. This chapter explores Bangladesh's rich cultural heritage, especially intangible and creative, through which the people of Bangladesh forge national identity, superimposing their flavoured representation of the country, its culture, language, religion, arts and crafts on a historical landscape. The media seizes on and publicizes results of tangible, intangible and creative cultural heritage study in blazing nationalist colour. There is little recognition that the normative standard of national identity in Bangladesh has repeatedly shifted its ground from Islam before 1971 to Bengali language and culture in 1971, and then back to Islam between 1977 and 1987 and now again back to Bengali language and culture from 2009 to date. Exploring Bangladesh's cultural heritage is therefore an ideal case study to illustrate how heritage serves the nation's interests in creating "an imagined political community that is imagined as both inherently limited and sovereign" (Anderson 1983: 7). Unfortunately, this is antithetical to science, because in the construction of the imagined political community, "the cultural shreds and patches used by nationalism are often arbitrary historical invention. Any old shred would have served as well. But in no way does it follow that the principle of nationalism … is itself in the least contingent [or] accidental" (Gellner 1983: 56).

When heritage experts and managers are entangled in the production of national identity in Bangladesh, they are effectively asked to choose Islam or Bengali language and culture as interpretive frameworks. This is problematic, particularly because heritage reifies ethnic and regional differences in the political and public imagination. This is also ironic because an anthropologist's overarching goal is to disseminate the fact that "language, religion, even skin colour, are not primary and definitional characteristics, but are social identifiers which are the result, the product, of struggles in the first place" (McCrone 1998: 28). Hence, it is necessary to see national identity more as a "process of becoming rather than being" (Hall 1996: 4), as a verb rather than as a noun, "as a concern with 'routes' rather than 'roots'" (McCrone 1998: 34). Consequently, 'nationalism' is a fluid construction, always in formation, always in flux, unfinished, reforming and reformulating. Heritage researchers in Bangladesh contribute to the on-going process of narrating the nation because interpretations of micro-heritage are always in flux, unfinished, reforming and reformulating. The goal of this chapter is to explore micro-heritage in Bangladesh, avoiding any projection of the present nation, its origins or identity, on a distant past. Micro-heritage resources continue to be of great significance to a sustainable development planning vision for Bangladesh. Heritage preservation and conservation, especially in developing countries like Bangladesh with growing populations, has depended heavily on the support from local communities.

This chapter highlights strategies for community-based outreach programmes to promote sustainable tourism as well as to stimulate public interest in micro-heritage preservation and management for socio-economic development of the local community using Bhitargarh as a case study. It also focuses on how types of micro-heritage provide a sense of identity to the local community; how they reflect and shape the social, religious, cultural, political and economic milieu of Bhitargarh in particular, and Bangladesh in general; how micro-heritage tourism can be more meaningful and responsible to society by appreciating culture and traditions and in what ways micro-heritage tourism becomes an effective tool to improve social benefits and participation for protecting and safeguarding cultural heritage of Bangladesh.

2.2   BANGLADESH

2.2.1   Geography and Environment

Bangladesh gained independence from Pakistan in 1971 and is wedged between the Indian states of West Bengal, Assam, Meghalaya, Tripura and Mizoram, with a border strip shared with Myanmar on the south-east. Its southern coast is open to the Bay of Bengal and, physiographically, most of Bangladesh's landmass is flat, comprised of a moribund delta, stabilized delta, active floodplains and a tidal delta that lie in the central and southern parts. A section of the north is a sandy alluvial fan; a basin of large lake-like bodies (haors) lies in the north-east; and three Pleistocene terraces lie in the north (the Barind Tract), the centre (the Madhupur Tracts) and the east (the Tippera Surface). Hilly regions are restricted to the Chittagong Belt in the south-east and a tiny section of the Sylhet Range to the north-east. A vast amount of water flows through Bangladesh's three principal river systems: the Ganga-Padma, Brahmaputra-Jamuna and Surma-Meghna.

To a large extent, geography exerts significant influences on the people of Bangladesh and their cultural practices, particularly as it gave rise to the tropical monsoon climate. Tropical wet evergreen and semi-evergreen forest biomes exist in the north-eastern hills and in the Chittagong hill tracts of south-eastern Bangladesh. The latter cover approximately 10% of Bangladesh and this area is particularly rich in wildlife, representing a global centre of biodiversity (Miah 2012). The central and north-western areas of the country are home to tropical moist deciduous forests and there are tropical littoral and mangrove forests in the coastal belt, the Sundarbans. The tropical deciduous forests are home to more than 220 species of animals while the Sundarbans represent the largest contiguous mangrove forest in the world, with 25 species of mangrove and many other forest products useful to humans and countless species of fish in the Bay of Bengal (Chowdhury et al. 2014: 7).

2.2.2   Population

The landmass of Bangladesh covers 147,610 square kilometres and is home to 160 million people with a population density of 964 per square kilometre in 2011. The majority population is homogeneous Bengalis (98%) and the remaining two per cent includes ethnic tribal populations and non-Bengali Muslims (Islam and Shamal 2011: 285; Bangladesh Population Census 2001). Bangladesh is predominantly an agricultural country and households rely on four principal livelihoods: agriculture/forestry/livestock (29.2%), agricultural labour (20.6%), business (14.7%) and salary/wage (10.9%). Almost 90% of Bangladesh's population is Muslim, with 9.2% Hindu, and the remainder representing Buddhists, Christians, and others (Bangladesh Population Census 2001; Islam and Shamal 2011: 287).

2.3   MICRO-HERITAGE OF BANGLADESH

Bangladesh has a rich micro-heritage and traditional culture that is integral to the everyday life of its people. Their knowledge, ideas, creative works have evolved from utilitarian and intellectual practices over thousands of years and form a variety of micro-heritage of indigenous performances, traditional games, ritual beliefs and practices, culinary art, fairs and festivals and traditional arts and crafts. These are powerful manifestations of social and cultural life of Bangladeshi people. Bangladeshis love music and dance, and indigenous performances are very popular for religious, educational and other secular purposes. About 100 genres of indigenous performances are related to various religions (Hinduism, Buddhism, Islam, and Christianity) and cults (Krishna and Chaitanya, Ramachandra, Siva and Kali, Manasa, and Nath) as well as a large number of secular performances (Ahmed 2000). Storytellers of indigenous performances in Bangladesh have no written text for memorizing but improvise their narratives while performing and employing the rhetorical tactics and strategies of their tradition and using words of their own. Similarly, the vernacular builder has no drawn plans; he has memories of buildings, familiar practices, reliable tools, tested skills and improvises constantly in the construction of a new house.

Traditional games are a popular pastime of the youngsters and there are more than 100 traditional games with rich culture involved in them. There are wide varieties of fairs and festivals, with ideological, religious as well as social functions. Village fairs also provide a balance between income-generation, sound-management of heritage and community involvement as all stakeholders participate. One interesting festival is Mangal Shobhajatra held during 14th April as part of the Bengali New Year celebration. Organized by the students and teachers of the Faculty of Fine Arts, University of Dhaka, who create animal and bird masks to drive away evil forces and people of all castes, creeds, religions, gender and age join the procession. Bengalis are fond of food (Ahmed 2007: 217–225) and prepare many dishes of fish, rice pies or pithas and varieties of sweets; of these, *Nakshi Pitha* is noteworthy.

Creative heritage or handicrafts of Bangladesh are also rich and varied and artists involved in making objects have a distinct nomenclature based on the material/medium they use. For example, bamboo object makers are known as Bash Sayal, cane object makers are Bet Sayal, potters are Kumar, Conch-shell object makers are Shankhari, fabrics weavers are Tanti or Jola, fibre weavers are Tantu-Bai, grass weavers are Ghash-Bai, leaf item producers are Pata Sayal, leather object producers are Chamar, metal craft artists and smiths of all kinds are Shekra, Kansari or Kansaru, shola or sponge wood object makers are Karandikar or Malakar, and carpenters are Sutar, respectively. The majority of artisans rely on ordinary communities for their familial, social and religious needs.

Bangladesh is blessed with alluvial resources formed from the silt deposits carried down by the Ganga, Brahmaputra and Meghna rivers, which gives very fine clay. Bangladeshi potters use simple techniques for pot making, and handmade pottery is still predominantly woman's art. Women of the Kumar and Patua castes make dolls and toys through pressing and moulding. Large jars are usually made by men and Mangalghat (auspices vases), Lakshmighat (auspices vase of the goddess Lakshmi), Mancha (an earthen stage for religious and medicinal plants), Shakher Hari (marriage ritual vessel), and various types of dolls are some of the specialized products that have distinct designs.

The men who weave jamdani saris on the banks of the Sitalakshya River in Narayanganj District prefer to weave the designs they learned in childhood, absorbing them into their growth, learning them as they learned their native tongue. The intangible and creative cultural heritage or micro-heritage of the country is handed on by word of mouth, by verbal instruction and example, by demonstration, or by custom and practice. This means that micro-heritage is passed on with little change from generation to generation. Micro-heritage thus serves as symbols of identity in communities and is an important source of national or local pride.

Fairs, festivals and rituals together made up congenial milieu in which the artisans work, the performers play and the common people participate in numerous games and sports, according to the taste and time of seasons. In rural Bangladesh, there is little distinction between a buyer and a seller as everybody is producing something to survive. The artisan/performer is a farmer and the farmer is his customer and, in the evening, they might play *Kabaddi* or *Hadudu* or perform Satya Pirer Gan together. Due to modernization, these cultural heritages are under threat but, despite this, there is great potential for the development of micro-heritage tourism.

2.4   BHITARGARH ARCHAEOLOGICAL SITE

Bhitargarh, meaning the 'inner fort', is located about 16 kilometres north-east of the town of Panchagarh, meaning the 'five forts', in Panchagarh District, the northern-most administrative district of Bangladesh. It is the largest fortified settlement to have been discovered in Bangladesh and extends over an area of about 25 square kilometres (Fig. 2.1). Interestingly, the site is actually trans-national as portions of its outer enclosures on the north, north-west and north-east lie in Jalpaiguri District of India's state of West Bengal. According to local traditions, the ruined city of Bhitargarh was once the capital city of King Prithu, known to the local community as the Maharaja. When Francis

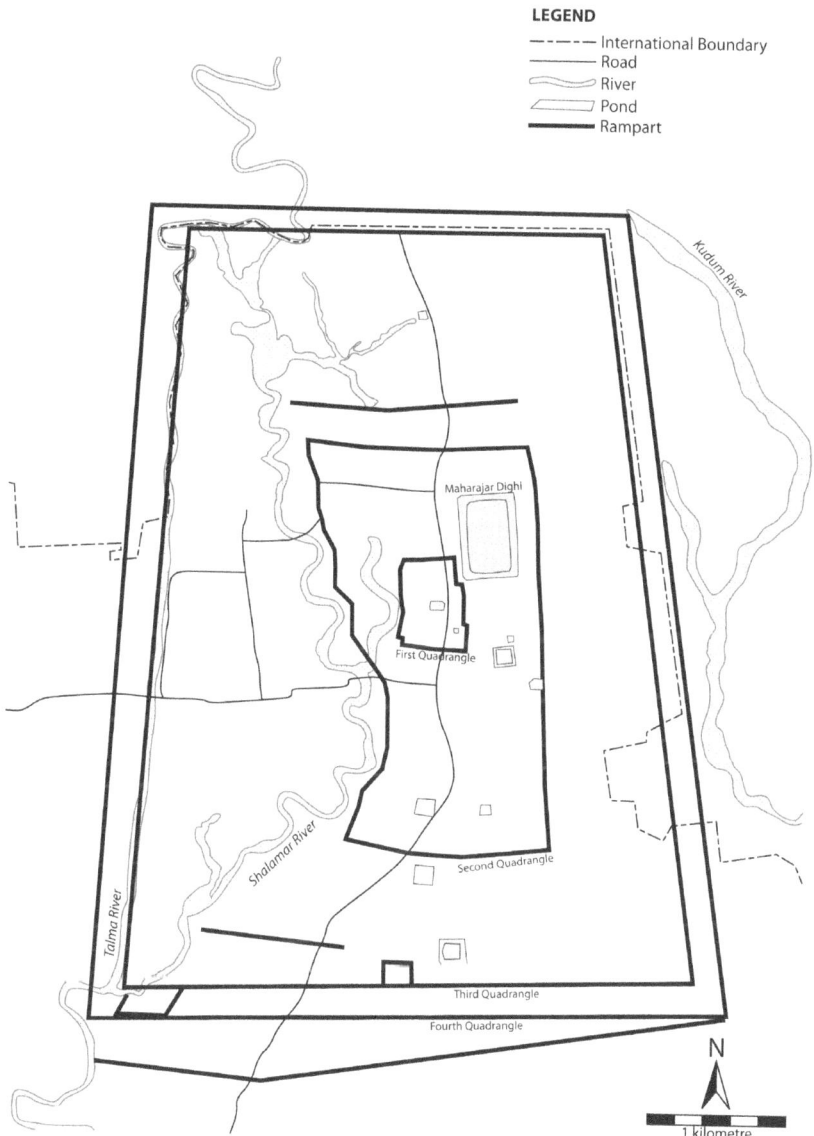

Fig. 2.1 Plan of the archaeological site of Bhitargarh

Buchanan visited the site in the nineteenth century, he found that local Hindus considered Prithu Raja "a very holy personage, who was so much afraid of having his purity sullied, that, on the approach of an abominable tribe of impure feeders named Kichok, he threw himself into a tank, and was followed by all his guards, so that the town was given up to plunder and the family ceased to reign" (Martin 1838: 406).

Bhitargarh lies on the Old Himalayan Piedmont Plain and is covered by sands and gravels carried down the Himalayan foothills at the end of the last glaciations when monsoon rainfall accompanied by Himalayan glacial meltwater gave rise to enormous water flows. The gravel beds of the site, which are a part of the Panchagarh sandy-gravel beds belonging to the Upper Pleistocene series, "are overlain by the Holocene series represented by alluvium and sometimes-fine sand, silt and clay" (Chowdhury 2003: 13). The gravels of the Holocene series are quite large and are alternated with very coarse to medium sand, "have quartz, quartzite, granite, gneiss and schist as their dominant lithologies" and their composition "is identical with that of the Daling series of the Himalayas" (Chowdhury 2003: 13). The topsoil of the site, known as Black Terai soil, is very dark grey or black in colour and extends over a thickness of 25 centimetres or more. At places, where the topsoil extends to 90 centimetres, a well-oxidized cambic B-horizon lies under it. At places, the texture of the soil is loamy sand but over most of the landscape, it is sandy clay loam (Ibrahim 2003: 36).

The major hydrographic determinants of the site are two rivers that originate in the Indian District of Jalpaiguri, namely the Talma in the west and Kudum in the east; both are tributaries of the Karatoya. The present course of the Teesta River is 11.85 kilometres east from the eastern rampart of the fourth quadrangle, while the Salmara River flows immediately outside the western rampart of the second quadrangle. The maximum temperature of the region is 30.2 °C and minimum is 10.1 °C, and annual rainfall is 2931 millimetres. The main crops grown here are paddy, jute, wheat, sugarcane, potato, groundnut, linseed, sesame, chilli and onion. Some extinct and nearly extinct crops are savory, millet, tobacco, *arahar* (pulse), *aus* and *kaun* paddy, and *dhemsi*. The main fruits are mango, papaya, jackfruit, guava, banana, pomegranate, pineapple, custard apple, betel nut and watermelon. Among the domestic animals, cows and goats are predominant. Tea gardens have recently been established in many areas within the site and the *sal* forest of Bhitargarh is also noteworthy.

The first systematic archaeological investigation of Bhitargarh was initiated in 2008 and conducted by the University of Liberal Arts Bangladesh (ULAB) under the direction of the author. At that time, the site was in a poor state of preservation and there was on-going encroachment and destruction. Since then, archaeological explorations and excavations have revealed that the city was enclosed within four concentric quadrangles, created with earth as well as brick ramparts. Rectangular bastions or buttresses, spaced at regular intervals, are integrated in the ramparts, apparently to strengthen the construction. Each quadrangle is surrounded by its own moat and excavations have revealed the foundations of religious and secular monuments. The excavated materials, pottery, clay objects, iron objects, brass objects, copper and gold Bangles, terracotta beads, stone beads, fragments of stone sculptures suggest a date range of between the seventh and twelfth century CE. In addition, there are ten 'dighis' or ponds that serviced the site in ancient time; the Maharajar Dighi, Kabarguri Dighi, Phulpukuri, Kodal Dhoya Dighi, Bara Malani Dighi, Choto Malani Dighi, Singari Dighi, Baghpukuri, and Jhaljhali Dighi. Of these, the Maharajar Dighi covers an area of 53 acres and is augmented with ten brick-paved bathing *ghat*s and brick-cased embankments. Evidence of dams has also been discovered, indicating that ancient inhabitants of Bhitargarh developed an ingenious system of irrigation and cultivation. The importance of Bhitargarh primarily lay in trade because of its strategic position on the ancient overland and riverine routes connecting Tibet, Sikkim, Nepal, Bhutan, Assam, Koch Bihar and the regions of the middle and lower Ganga valleys (Jahan 2011: 449–482).

Bhitargarh contains immense potential in terms of history and heritage of Bangladesh in particular, and South Asia in general. Furthermore, its archaeological heritage along with its natural beauty and various types of intangible and creative heritage gives Bhitargarh the potential for sustainable cultural and eco-tourism. However, the site is under threat as, despite a High Court ruling prohibiting damage and modern construction works within the site, local inhabitants continue to encroach the ancient city (Fig. 2.2). Currently, some 40,000 people live today within the ancient city of Bhitargarh; most are migrants from other parts of Bangladesh, from the Districts of Comilla, Rangpur, Tangail and Mymensingh, or recently settled and a small number arrived from the Indian District of Jalpaiguri. Both agriculture and agriculture labour remain the main source of income. As most people arrived here

Fig. 2.2 Excavations demonstrating the presence of archaeological monuments within gardens at Bhitagarh

from different areas, they do not have close association with the heritage of the site and, in their endeavour to extend cultivation and habitation, have caused considerable damage to the site, so the archaeological remains of this ancient city are gradually disappearing. In addition, most land within the site is privately owned except for a little owned by the Government. The Department of Archaeology does not possess any land nor do they have any projects at the site. Therefore, to protect the archaeological heritage site of Bhitargarh, there is no other option left other than community engagement.

2.5   COMMUNITY ENGAGEMENT

We have employed a number of community engagement strategies to raise the awareness of the inhabitants of Bhitargarh of their cultural heritage, and increase their participation in its preservation and conservation. For example, seminars, workshops and discussion forums have been organized at the site at which the author offered her findings, shared her vision and engaged in a dialogue with local academics, journalists and villagers in order to stimulate public interest in heritage preservation and commemorations of the past. These meetings also served to explore public memory and localized heritage, while signboards displaying heritage awareness slogans were erected at strategic points in the villages, including on structural remains, in order to enhance public education. Local inhabitants, especially the landowners of the excavation sites, and women and children, have been trained in archaeological excavation techniques to make it possible for them to be a part of the excavation team and thus stake a rightful claim to their own heritage. Approaches were thus developed to safeguard archaeological heritage and promote sustainable tourism as well as stimulate community interest in archaeological heritage preservation and management for socio-economic development of the local community.

As a part of the research project, the team decided to investigate the living traditions and cultures of Bhitargarh to understand the micro-heritage of the people who live today within the ancient city. Linking this with the archaeology is important for employment and income-generation through, for example, the production and sale of local micro-heritage products. Awareness programmes were required to deliver seminars, workshops, trainings, discussion forums, focus group discussions and meetings to help understand how the community defined the authenticity of their heritage. In addition, a seven-day "Bhitargarh Festival" has been organized each February–March each year to allow the community to exhibit their tangible, intangible and creative cultural heritage and celebrate the discoveries to date. A total of 30,000 people attended the festival, which cost only £9130 to organize.

2.6   Bhitargarth Festival

The first step was to organize meetings and seminars with social and administrative groups, such as school teachers, journalists, union council chairman and members, local youths and community police to share the idea of Bhitargarh Festival and develop the programme. All villagers were then informed, and the work of organizing the festival began. Key to this process was the formation of an Organizing Committee of 65 people with representatives from all local groups. A variety of programmes were then designed for the 2017 Bhitargarh Festival to cater to the needs of local school children, their parents and communities and arrange activities that reflected their own culture and traditions. This resulted in the participation of 4000 students from 26 educational institutions (school, college and madrasah) in drawing, debates, instant speech, and recitation, dance and music competitions. To relate the festival to the archaeological remains, we arranged swimming competitions in the Maharajar Dighi, Hans Khela (duck game) in Phulpukuri and fishing in Malani as well as the Maharajar Dighi. There were inter-ward tournaments of indigenous games among the villagers and photography of the archaeological, natural, intangible and creative heritage of Bhitargarh were exhibited to highlight the values of their own culture.

Indigenous performances were organized both for their safeguarding and social awareness building, some of which were held at night. Of these, Satya Pirer Gan, very popular at Bhitargarh, is a genre of performance given at rural homesteads of greater Dinajpur and Rajshahi Districts to propitiate Satya Pir and earn his blessings for overcoming physical illness, attaining wealth, or bearing children. Satya Pir is a mythic saint and among Hindus, he is known as Satyanarayan, an incarnation of Vishnu. Satya Pirer Gan is performed by faqirs of Satya Pir and his disciples and devotees, who are offered oblation of sweet (*shirni*) and money at the end of performance. The faqirs are usually low-caste Hindus as well as Muslims (Fig. 2.3). Lathi-Khela, a popular form of martial art in Bangladesh exhibiting skilled stick and footwork, was also demonstrated by two groups from Bhitargarh.

2.7   Conclusion

The Bhitargarh Festival allowed us to bring together as many of the communities living within the ancient site as possible. In addition to celebrating the site's tangible and intangible heritage, we also organized a village fair to sell villagers' household objects, ornamental or decorative objects, toys and indigenous food to generate income. Some villagers also arranged parking facilities, toilet facilities, restaurants and tea-stalls to meet visitors' needs and generate additional income. Local van drivers were also in demand as every day thousands of visitors came to participate during the festival. As a result, the celebration of Bhitargarh's heritage allowed many people to earn money from the festival. These points help us understand that traditions, culture and heritage are not luxuries for the people of Bhitargarh but are touchstones of identity.

Fig. 2.3 Performance of Satya Pirer Gan during the Bhitargarh Festival

Clearly, the interest of the state in promoting cultural heritage of Bangladesh has been to forge a national identity by superimposing the current representation of the country obtained through territorial and demographic signs on a cultural landscape and thus claim authenticity for the nation. Cultural historians in Bangladesh must promote awareness that our contribution to narrating the nation is an on-going process, always in flux, unfinished, and reforming. Of critical importance is that we celebrate the micro as well as the macro-heritage.

REFERENCES

Ahmed, S. J. (2000). *Achinpakhi Infinity: Indigenous Theatre of Bangladesh.* Dhaka: University Press.
Ahmed, W. (2007). *Folk Arts.* Dhaka: Asiatic Society of Bangladesh.
Anderson, B. (1983). *Imagined Communities: Reflections on the Origin and Spread of Nationalism.* London: Verso.
Bangladesh Population Census 2001. (2005). Dhaka: Bangladesh Bureau of Statistics.

Chowdhury, S. Q. (2003). Hardrock. In I. Sirajul (Ed.), *Banglapedia: National Encyclopedia of Bangladesh* (Vol. 5, pp. 12–14). Dhaka: Asiatic Society of Bangladesh.

Chowdhury, M. S. H., Izumiyama, S., & Koike, M. (2014). Introduction. In M. S. H. Chowdhury (Ed.), *Forest Conservation in Protected Areas of Bangladesh: Policy and Community Development Perspectives* (pp. 1–22). New York: Springer.

Gellner, E. (1983). *Nations and Nationalism*. Oxford: Basil Blackwell.

Hall, S. (1996). Introduction: Who Needs Identity? In S. Hall & P. DuGay (Eds.), *Questions of Cultural Identity* (pp. 1–17). London: Sage.

Ibrahim, A. M. (2003). Bangladesh Soil. In I. Sirajul (Ed.), *Banglapedia: National Encyclopedia of Bangladesh* (Vol. 2, pp. 32–37). Dhaka: Asiatic Society of Bangladesh.

Islam, M. A., & Shamal, C. K. (2011). Population. In I. Sirajul (Ed.), *Banglapedia: National Encyclopedia of Bangladesh* (Vol. 11, pp. 284–295). Dhaka: Asiatic Society of Bangladesh.

Jahan, S. H. (2011). Archaeological Explorations and Excavations at Bhitargarh (2008–2011). In Harun-or-R. (Ed.), *Diamond Jubilee Volume of the Journal of the Asiatic Society of Bangladesh* (pp. 449–482). Dhaka: Asiatic Society of Bangladesh.

Martin, M. (1838). *The History, Antiquities, Topography and Statistics of Eastern India, Comprising the Districts of Behar, Shahabad, Bhagulpoor, Goruckpoor, Dinajepoor, Purniya, Ronggopoor, and Assam*. London: W.H. Allen.

McCrone, D. (1998). *The Sociology of Nationalism: Tomorrow's Ancestors*. London: Routledge.

Miah, M. (2012). *Evolution Report of Community-Based Participatory Herbal Gardens*. Dhaka: Arannyak Foundation.

CHAPTER 3

Awakening Myths, Legends and Heritage

K. Krishnan and Vrushab Mahesh

Abstract K. Krishnan and Vrushab Mahesh focus on the design and development of the Bindu Sarovar Museum at Sidhpur in the Indian State of Gujarat. A *sristhal* or pious place, Sidhpur is considered one of the holiest Hindu sites to perform *shradha* or post-funerary rites for one's mother. In this context, a group of academics, religious practioners, policy makers and community stakeholders came together to fashion a modern museum, which presents myth, legend and religious and ritual practices. Drawing from the site's deep intangible heritage traditions, this chapter will evaluate whether this development met its stated goals of satisfying the intellectual curiosity of visitors, developed their sense of the past and awareness of heritage of the region and, finally, is providing opportunities to generate income for resident populations.

Keywords India · Sidhpur · Museum · Death ritual

K. Krishnan (✉) · V. Mahesh
Department of Archaeology and Ancient History, The Maharaja Sayajirao University of Baroda, Vadodara, India

© The Author(s) 2019
R. Coningham and N. Lewer (eds.), *Archaeology, Cultural Heritage Protection and Community Engagement in South Asia*,
https://doi.org/10.1007/978-981-13-6237-8_3

3.1   Introduction

Heritage and tradition have long been recognised as significant determinants in the formulation of identities within contemporary rural and urban societies across South Asia. However, entities characterised as tangible or intangible have often been treated separately as if they are broadly perceived to have little or no interlink with each other. Closer reflection reveals that there is actually a complex and pervasive interplay between both these components along with the landscapes and communities in which they are situated. In this context, contemporary practices and approaches involving the preservation of heritage have displayed a tendency to greatly emphasise tangible entities and advocate their heightened legal and physical protection. Such practices have also tended to promote perceptions that associated intangible practices can be destructive and cause irreversible damage to, or transformation of, sites and monuments. As a result, heritage policymakers and managers frequently recommend the demarcating and fencing of arbitrary areas around tangible entities. Although successful to a large degree in reducing direct physical damage to the monuments and sites, such practices have culminated in restricting access to the site's local communities, who often draw their identities, and own intangible practices, from those same tangible entities.

There is also awareness across South Asia that there is increasing conflict between the necessity and will to preserve heritage and the need for socio-economic development through the enhancement of facilities and services, and the construction of mega-infrastructure. Under such circumstances, sites and monuments, the tangible entities of heritage, often receive greater attention, while intangible components and the local populations who live in close vicinity to the tangible entities, are ignored. Although existing legislation necessitates mediation between different stakeholders and the subsequent resettlement of the populations affected during the implementation of infrastructure development, local communities and their intangible practices rarely directly benefit from such undertakings (Fisher 1995; Rajgopal 2005: 345–359; Levien 2006: 3581–3583).

Referencing some key examples of the former interventions, this chapter will provide a very different example of infrastructure development linked to intangible practices rather than static tangible entities, the design and development of the Bindu Sarovar Museum at

Sidhpur in the Indian State of Gurarat. A *sristhal* or 'pious place', Sidhpur is considered one of the holiest Hindu sites to perform *shradha* or post-funerary rites for one's mother. In this context, a group of academics, religious practitioners, policymakers and community stakeholders came together to fashion a modern museum, which presents myth, legend and religious and ritual practices. Drawing from the site's deep intangible heritage traditions, this chapter will evaluate whether this development met its stated goals of satisfying the intellectual curiosity of visitors, developed their sense of the past and awareness of heritage of the region and, finally, is providing opportunities to generate income for resident populations.

3.2 COMMUNITY, HERITAGE AND MEGA-INFRASTRUCTURE

While attention has been increasingly focused on the very real human and cultural impacts of the development of Pakistan's Orange Metro Line in Lahore, the apparent shift of balance from the necessity of heritage protection towards the necessity of the implementation of mega-infrastructure for public good has long been present within South Asia. Indeed, in India, such decisions have been acutely visible during the implementation of major infrastructure projects in the region for decades. Significant examples in this regard, may be drawn to the two highly culturally important Buddhist sites, Nagarjunakonda in Andhra Pradesh and Devnimori in Gujarat, India. The former was one of the capitals of the Iksvaku dynasty, who ruled much of the eastern Krishna Valley between the third and fourth centuries CE (Chakrabarti 1995: 306). Established across an already ancient landscape beside the River Krishna, the site comprised a fortified citadel and hinterland, rich in civic monuments, Hindu temples and over 30 Buddhist monasteries. In comparison, the fourth to seventh century CE complex of Devnimori, on the bank of the River Meshwo, included two monasteries, four votive stupas and an apsidal temple focused on a brick built stupa with a base of almost 26 metres square (Mehta and Chowdhary 1966).

Despite the significance of both sites, yielding as they did reliquaries believed to hold relics of the Buddha (Mitra 1971), as the region surrounding these heritage sites were characterised by dry climates and irregular rainfall, government agencies decided to construct dams across the Krishna and Meshvo to facilitate storage and irrigation. The Krishna was damned by the world's largest masonry dam, forming the 285 square kilometre water sheet known as the Nagarjuna Sagar. Generating hydroelectric power and irrigating 5300 square kilometres, M. Gopal Rao dedicated an entire volume to this mega-infrastructure, pointedly entitled *The Epic of a Great Temple of Humanity* (1979). As the project led to complete submergence of the site's ancient temples and monuments, and the landscape in which they were situated, rescue archaeological surveys and excavations were undertaken between 1954 and 1960 by the Archaeological Survey of India (ASI) (*Indian Archaeology: A Review* 1954–1955: 30; 1955–1956: 23–26; 1956–1957: 5–10, 35–38, 58–59; 1959–1960: 5–10; 1960–1961: 1). Some monuments were excavated and then reconstituted on an island of higher ground formed by the Nagarjuna Sagar, although they were described as "replicas" (Krishna Murthy 1977: 2).

Started in 1959 and completed in 1972, the dam across the Meshwo generated a rather smaller, yet important water body of 11.16 square kilometres. Like at Nagarjunakonda, the decision to flood the reservoir meant that the ancient monastic complex at Devnimori would also be submerged and thus was also subject to rescue excavations and survey led by the Department of Archaeology and Ancient History of the Maharaja Sayajirao University of Baroda (*Indian Archaeology: A Review* 1960–1961: 9–11; 1961–1962: 12–13; 1962–1963: 8; Mehta and Chowdhary 1966; Schastok 1985: 23–27). Investigated and documented, most of the remains were left in situ, while limited numbers of carved brick and more exceptional remains were removed. Although, these exceptional operations were necessitated by the need of the hour, in retrospect it is clear that the links between these culturally significant tangible entities with the landscape was lost. Instead, elements of these significant monuments were mostly stored within the premises of the agencies, who had undertaken the archaeological operations, or they were selectively exhibited as part of museum collections.

As significantly, there were also few attempts to identify the manner in which their local communities articulated their identities with the ruins. Indeed, little has been done to study the impact of the intangible practices of the communities impacted by this mega-infrastructure, which resulted in the partial submergence of 13 villages and the full loss of six around Devnimori and 54 villages at Nagarjunakonda. On the centenary of the ASI in 1961, Prime Minister Jawaharlal Nehru made his decision-making clear by stating that:

a matter of conscience arose for us when we were considering what we should do about Nagarjunakonda...There was this buried city gradually coming out, and there was the proposal to erect a dam there and create a big reservoir which would supply water for irrigation. There was a direct conflict between the claims of today in the sense of practical utility and the claims of the past. We were troubled by the conflict. But it was inevitable that we should decide ultimately in favour of the present. (Nehru 1964)

3.3   SIDHPUR

In recent years, the global role of museum in the sphere of heritage preservation has extended beyond their traditional character. They are now transforming into forerunners in education, preservation and the presentation of both tangible and intangible elements of heritage, but also offering the means to foster identities and investigate into the manner in which the identities are drawn from heritage. Such developments have been a result of the intellectual exercises that have taken place in the discipline of museum studies over the years across the globe (Walsh 1992; Kaplan 1994). In South Asia, museums range significantly in terms of their size and expertise, along with their primary nature of their exhibits and target audiences. Thus, some museums focus on highlighting specific issues, for instance textile craft, while other museums catering to a wider audience and have within their exhibits a range of antiquities/artefacts drawn from different regions. In addition, there are also 'craftparks', which serve as 'living museums' and site museums associated with archaeological sites which serve as induction and interaction centres. Despite their varying nature, they all continue to play a vital role in the dissemination of knowledge to a wider audience. However, despite the wide range of focus covered by museums across South Asia, until recently there were no museums highlighting the nature of intangible and oral traditions and mythology within the specific landscape in which they have been hosted for centuries. This avenue becomes particularly acute as it has been observed in the South Asian narrative, that community identities are very often drawn from local histories, cultural practices and belief systems, which are in most cases associated with either the tangible remains or a specific geographic and cultural landscape. This case study will now highlight the challenges faced in developing a museum at Sidhpur, Gujarat, India, that focused on presenting the mythology, legends and heritage associated with the centre and the region while also taking into account the intellectual curiosity of the local population and the pilgrims who visit this centre for the performance of specific rituals.

The modern town of Sidhpur is situated on the banks of River Saraswati in Patan District, Gujarat, India. Historically it was known as *sristhal*, 'a pious place' (Burgess 1874: 19). Among the religious Hindus, it is also known as *Matrugaya* and is considered as one the holiest venues to perform the *shradha* or the post-funerary rites for one's mother. This practice is drawn from the mythical belief of Parsurama having beheaded his mother and performed her *shradha* at Sidhpur upon his father Jamadagni's instructions, who further revived his mother as per his request. Sidhpur is also considered important as it is believed to be the birthplace of sage Kapila, one of the founders of the Sankhya philosophical tradition. The other significant cultural centres within Sidhpur, include the ruins of the twelfth Century CE Rudra Mahalaya temple, the fifteenth century CE Jami Masjid and the *havelis* of the Dawoodi Bohras.

3.4   CONCEIVING THE BINDU SAROVAR MUSEUM

An idea of setting up a museum at Siddhpur was conceived by Shri Jayanarayan Vyas, Honourable Minister of Health, Sports, Culture, Pilgrimage and Tourism, Government of Gujarat, India, towards the latter half of 2010 to propagate religious tourism within the region by presenting local myths and legends. He planned to achieve this by incorporating many dimensions of the past, culture, history and society within the region and also outside of it. One of the key intentions behind the setting up of the museum at Siddhpur was to informally educate the people about the cultural significance of the region in order that they develop a sense of past. Generating such awareness was, in turn, hoped to enable the protection of heritage from destruction, which is taking place in the region as a part of modernization. In addition, it had to also be geared towards satisfying the intellectual curiosity of human mind and generating economy for local communities through rituals and tourism.

During initial surveys, it became clear to our team of a group of academics, religious practitioners, policymakers and community stakeholders that local legends and traditions had an antiquity stretching back many years. Interestingly, many had also been transformed to regionalize them, whereby localities and rivers within and around the township were identified and named after religiously and culturally significant ones. This was interesting as it revealed that the population of Sidhpur during the past also had had an interest in their antiquity, especially attached to religious sentiments. Myths and legends often assign specific religious significance to any place and situate any place within the wider circuit of religious pilgrimage. Many times, paucity of funds, lack of transportation facilities or old age, hinders the movement of pilgrims to distant sacred centres. Such difficulties led to the promotion of other centres as hubs of pilgrimage by merely assigning and associating specific myths and legends to them, thereby altering their character. Thus, as myth and legends form an integral aspect of South Asian societies, recognizing their importance and generating a rational understanding of them within the current society through any mechanism is an arduous task.

The presence of several myths was one of the key challenges encountered while developing the academic rationale for the museum. Although its documentation could be undertaken with the help of textual sources such as *Dharmasastras, Garuda Purana, Vishnu Purana, Vayu Purana, Narada Purana* in corroboration with their local perceptions and interpretations, it was necessary to also devise means to present an intangible component in a tangible manner before an audience of various socio-economic and educational strata. Further, as Sidhpur is significantly associated with the performance of *shradha* sacrifice for one's mother, it became increasingly challenging to portray such themes within the confines of a museum. In addition, as the museum had to cater to the intellectual curiosities of a diverse nature of visitors, it was also necessary to incorporate artefacts and collections along with their replicas, if needed, that highlighted the history and antiquity of the region.

Thus the development of the Bindu Sarovar Museum at Sidhpur was guided by three significant co-designed goals:

- to satisfy the intellectual curiosity of visitors;
- to develop a sense of the past and awareness of heritage of the region amongst visitors;
- and to provide opportunities to generate new economic benefits for the local population.

This demanded the inclusion of religious and ritualistic elements, along with those of history and society. Therefore, three galleries, *Thirth*, *Itihas* and *Samaj* were created. The first gallery focussed on the religious and ritual practices being undertaken at Sidhpur, where the various myths and legends associated with the ritual of *shradha* are presented. As mentioned earlier, the preparation of the first gallery was most difficult in every spirit as the architecture had to match with the theme of the exhibit. As the ritual is associated with water, the concept of the museum would be incomplete without the presence of water as it is considered primordial. Primordial water is considered to be pure and it is also believed that the '*prana*', the element that gives life, originates and goes back to primordial water. Therefore the architecture of the gallery and the museum had to be designed in a manner that reflected the aforementioned theme. The second gallery included artefacts, collections, both original and replicas, and photographs acquired from different institutions and private collections that reflected the history of the region. These included collections from the Prehistoric period to the contemporary times. The third gallery highlighted the societal aspects of the populations which reside within the region. Furthermore, the museum complex also housed artefacts of the past and everyday life. In addition, a replica of the monumental gateway of the Rudra Mahalaya Temple complex was also constructed and is now housed within the museum premises.

3.5   DISCUSSION

As the desire to achieve a peaceful rest and the performance of funerary rituals has dominated the cultural thought of most South Asian societies, the above undertaking marks a novel approach at developing a museum with an extensive focus directed towards highlighting the myths and legends associated with the performance of death ritual in the centre. The significant feature of this undertaking involves catering to the intellectual curiosity of the visitors and the local communities, as the museum is housed in the same complex as the Bindu Sarovar, an artificial tank, where the ritual of *shradha* is practiced (Fig. 3.1). Furthermore, the planning team of the museum also took into account the legends recorded in literary records along with the local variations in order to incorporate the aspirations of the local communities. In addition, it also incorporates exhibits which highlight the region's history and culture with an aim to preserve heritage and promote heritage awareness amongst the visitors.

Fig. 3.1 The Bindu Sarovar at Sidhpur

The above undertaking is, however, characterised by a few shortcomings in their execution as the construction of the museum in close proximity to the sacred centre may alter the sacred landscape of the ancient *sristhal*. Furthermore, the setting up of modern replicas of ancient monuments/artefacts may also affect the perception of the visitors to the museum. A case here may be stressed upon the setting up of a modern replica of gateway of the Rudra Mahalaya temple within the premises of the museum complex. The debates surrounding the setting up of the replica centred upon the need to provide visual access of the monument to the visitors as the access to the original monument has been barred by government agencies (Fig. 3.2). Hence, it was felt that the setting up of a scaled replica of the monument is significant to allow visitors to gauge the intricacies of sculptural embellishments adorning the monument. Further, as Sidhpur is located within close proximity to Devnimori, the museum houses artefacts and the replica of the casket recovered from the excavations undertaken by the Department of Archaeology and Ancient History, the Maharaja Sayajirao University of Baroda. It also houses replica and original specimens of artefacts belonging to prehistoric and

Fig. 3.2 Replica of the Rudra Mahalaya Temple's Kirti Torana at the Bindu Sarovar Museum

protohistoric periods that were found from within this region. Although it may be debated that it is impossible to relocate the 'dislocated' past merely by placing artefacts and their replicas as museum exhibits, it should be noted that the fundamental aim of the museum is to generate an awareness of heritage and present before a wider audience about the rich antiquity of the region. The museum development team since the very early stages had to keep in mind that as it would mostly be pilgrims with limited time and awareness who visit the museum, the nature of exhibits should be in a manner that would enhance visitor experiences and not burden the visitor (Fig. 3.3).

3.6   Conclusion

This case study has demonstrated how modern infrastructure designed to augment and enhance a site rich in tangible and intangible heritage has attempted to balance the needs of pilgrims, visitors and residents as well as provide an enhanced venue with new streams of potential economic

Fig. 3.3 The Bindu Sarovar Museum

benefit. In contrast to the earlier examples of the clearing of communities and their practices from sites, the case study from Sidhpur has attempted to work with both to enhance the environment and experience. Attempting to avoid what Nehru referred to as "the direct conflict between the claims of today in the sense of practical utility and the claims of the past" (1964), both appear to have been approached equally. While the methodology involved in the conception and execution of the museum may be associated with certain shortcomings, it nevertheless marks a significant milieu in incorporating local communities and their beliefs within the sphere of heritage protection and awareness in the region of South Asia rather than relocating and dislocating such populations as in earlier cases. Completed in 2011, 96% of visitors to score it at TripAdvisor considered it to be either Excellent or Very Good   (https://www.tripadvisor.co.uk/Attraction_Review-g3317041-d7101961-Reviews-Bindu_Sarovar-Sidhpur_Patan_District_Gujarat.html), suggesting that its design was meeting its intention. Certainly, many of the comments indicate that this is the case: "We were very aware of a great respect in the Bindu Sarovar. It is a place where one helps their late mother attain liberation. We could not follow all the various steps and actions but everyone was quite happy to let us watch and try to learn. It is a duty but also a pleasure". Similar methods for developing a visitor centre are also currently being conceived at the UNESCO World Heritage Site of Champaner-Pavagadh Archaeological Park, Gujarat, India, that would include both tangible and intangible components of the site and thereby fulfil the intellectual curiosity and the aspirations of the local communities and visitors to the site. Finally, the authors would like to express their deep sense of gratitude to Shri Jayanarayan Vyas, former minister of Gujarat for conceiving the idea of the museum and Dr. Ashok Rajeshirke for his support in collecting the data.

REFERENCES

Burgess, J. (1874). *Photographs of Architecture and Scenery in Gujarat and Rajputana*. Bombay and Shimla: Bourne and Shepard.

Chakrabari, D. K. (1995). Post-Mauryan States of Mainland South Asia. In F. R. Allchin (Ed.), *The Archaeology of Early Historic South Asia: The Emergence of Cities and States* (pp. 274–325). Cambridge: Cambridge University Press.

Fisher, W. (Ed.). (1995). *Towards Sustainable Development? Struggling Over India's Narmada River*. New York: M.E. Shrape.

Indian Archaeology: A Review. (1954–1955). New Delhi: Archaeological Survey of India.

Indian Archaeology: A Review. (1955–1956). New Delhi: Archaeological Survey of India.

Indian Archaeology: A Review. (1956–1957). New Delhi: Archaeological Survey of India.

Indian Archaeology: A Review. (1958–1959). New Delhi: Archaeological Survey of India.

Indian Archaeology: A Review. (1959–1960). New Delhi: Archaeological Survey of India.

Indian Archaeology: A Review. (1960–1961). New Delhi: Archaeological Survey of India.

Indian Archaeology: A Review. (1961–1966). New Delhi: Archaeological Survey of India.

Indian Archaeology: A Review. (1962–1963). New Delhi: Archaeological Survey of India.

Kaplan, F. E. S. (Ed.). (1994). *Museums and the Making of Ourselves: The Role of Objects in National Identity*. London: Leicester University Press.

Krishna Murthy, K. (1977). *Nagarjunakonda: A Cultural Study*. New Delhi: Concept Publishing Company.

Levien, M. (2006). Narmada and the Myth of Rehabilitation. *Economic and Political Weekly, 41*(33), 3581–3585.

Mehta, R. N., & Chowdhary, S. N. (1966). *Excavation at Devnimori: A Report of the Excavation Conducted from 1960 to 1963.* Baroda: M.S. University of Baroda.

Mitra, D. (1971). *Buddhist Monuments.* Calcutta: Sahitya Samsad.

Nehru, J. (1964). *Jawaharlal Nehru Selected Speeches: Volume 4.* New Delhi: Ministry of Information & Broadcasting.

Rajagopal, B. (2005). The Role of Law in Counter-Hegemonic Globalization and Global Legal Pluralism: Lessons from the Narmada Valley Struggle in India. *Leiden Journal of International Law, 18,* 345–387.

Rao, M. G. (1979). *Nagarjuna Sagar: The Epic of a Great Temple of Humanity.* Bombay: Bharatiya Vidya Bhavan.

Schastok, S. L. (1985). *The Samalaji Sculptures and 6th Century Art in Western India.* Leiden: E.J. Brill.

Walsh, K. (1992). *The Representation of the Past: Museums and Heritage in the Post-modern World.* London: Routledge.

CHAPTER 4

Kuragala: Religious and Ethnic Communities in a Contested Sacred Heritage Site in Sri Lanka

Venerable Mahinda Deegalle

Abstract Deegalle describes the archaeology of, and analyses the religious controversies over, a contested sacred space - Kuragala in the central highlands of Sri Lanka. This case study illustrates the significant dangers facing monuments and archaeological sites in Sri Lanka and elsewhere from rapid development and encroachment. Drawing from literary accounts, administrative reports, archaeological surveys and anthropological observations, the chapter outlines the history of conflict between Buddhists and Muslims over this Prehistoric space. Deegalle examines the ways in which twentieth century Buddhist and Muslim identity is constructed in relation to Kuragala and explains Buddhist concerns over the Islamization of the site. This has political ramifications and affects harmonious and functional relationships both locally, and more widely in Sri Lanka, and points to the need for deeper community engagement.

V. M. Deegalle (✉)
Bath Spa University, Bath, UK
e-mail: m.deegalle@bathspa.ac.uk

© The Author(s) 2019
R. Coningham and N. Lewer (eds.), *Archaeology, Cultural Heritage Protection and Community Engagement in South Asia*,
https://doi.org/10.1007/978-981-13-6237-8_4

Keywords Kuragala · Sri Lanka · Identity · Heritage · Sufi Pilgrimage · Buddhists and Muslims

4.1   INTRODUCTION

Using historical analysis and primary data, this chapter examines the communal religious and ethnic tensions that have arisen in the context of the conservation, preservation and continual use of archaeological heritage in Sri Lanka. It focuses on one contested, mismanaged, religiously articulated and politically controversial sacred space, Kuragala. In the contestation, both contemporary Buddhists and Muslims, and those of the twentieth century, have been involved. This sacred space, contested on the grounds of ethnic and religious differentiation, has significant implications for the conservation of archaeological heritage in Sri Lanka as well as in sustaining religious and ethno-political harmony.

4.2   KURAGALA TODAY

Kuragala, whose name is derived from the Sinhala for 'hollow rock', is an ancient site whose origins can be associated with Buddhism. According to the Government of Sri Lanka's Department of Archaeology (DoA), it can be dated back to the second century BCE due to the presence of early Brahmi inscriptions (Collins 1932: 167). At the time, C.H. Collins also asserted that the site was significant and that "if properly explored, would yield other remains of interest" (ibid.: 168). His confidence was confirmed in 2013 when excavations provided evidence of prehistoric occupation and a field survey in 2014 recorded prehistoric tools on the northern slope of the hillock (Somadeva et al. 2015: 5–6) (Fig. 4.1).

While the archaeological and historic site comprises a rock shelter, the name 'Kuragala' is used here broadly to refer to the entire area. Located in Ratnapura District in Sri Lanka's Sabaragamuva Province, the shelter is on the edge of the Balangoda Plateau, 23 kilometres east of the town of Balangoda. The nearest village, Thanjantenna, is 1.5 kilometres away and has a population of Muslims and Buddhists, and a Buddhist temple.

Kuragala is an important sacred site, both historically and religiously, and two contemporary religious communities, Buddhist and Muslim, treasure their access. Kuragala's significance for Buddhists is due to its location on the ancient pilgrimage route from the south of the island to Sri Pada (Adam's Peak) (Deegalle 2018). Five early Brahmi inscriptions dating to the third century BCE, drip-ledged caves and remains

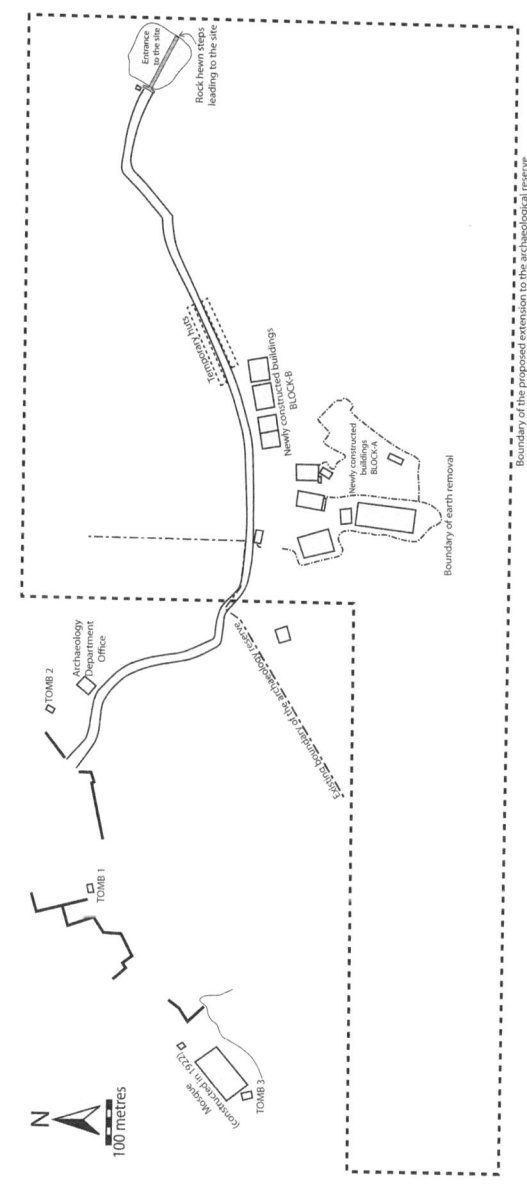

Fig. 4.1 Plan of the archaeological site of Kuragala

of a *stupa* provide additional archaeological evidence of Buddhist affiliation (Paranavitana 1970: 59). Kuragala's significance for Muslims derives from its link with the Persian Sufi mystic Muhyiuddin Abdul Qadir al-Gilani (1077–1166 CE), who is believed to have visited.

The approach road from the village was repaired in 2013 during a major reorganization of the site and ends in the valley in a car park. From here, pilgrims walk up a beautiful staircase carved into the rock, resembling rock-cut staircases in the ancient Buddhist complexes of Mihintale and Anuradhapura. Its 'unusual' feature is that access to the steps, recently inscribed with Muslim names, is through a large white entrance arch with green minarets. This flamboyant arch, with Islamic motifs, was constructed in 1982 (Aboosally 2002: 64). Some local residents identify this new construction as a Muslim 'Torana', (Fig. 4.2) the latter being a gate with a specific religious emphasis and designation usually associated with Buddhist sites.

After climbing the steps to a plateau, the path turns downwards through a line of shops. The plateau also hosts several buildings, including offices and quarters for the employees of the Daftar Gilani complex. There are temporary constructions in this area used during the annual Kanturi, or Kandoori, festival as well as a temporary police post. These new buildings were relocated here following the reorganization of the site in 2013. Before that, poorly constructed and unplanned buildings covered much of the area around the mosque. The remodelling, under the supervision of the Defense Secretary, was a government response to growing communal and religious tensions over competing claims to the site from the two communities. Specifically, it followed demands for immediate action from groups, such as the *Bodu Bala Sena* (The Army of Buddhist Power), the *Sinhala Ravaya* (The Sinhala Roar) and the *Jatika Hela Urumaya* (National Sinhala Heritage), a political party who only fielded Buddhist monks in the 2004 Parliamentary elections (Deegalle 2004).

In terms of legal jurisdiction, it would have been better if the Director-General of Archaeology had undertaken conciliatory measures to manage the emerging crises rather than the Defense Secretary. In the event, the Defense Secretary had discussions with the mosque trustees, resulting in the relocation. This intervention also enabled the DoA to conduct exploratory excavations, which discovered a prehistoric skeleton, as well as surveys of the area (Somadeva et al. 2015). Prior to 2013, the sacred site and the entire valley were dotted with buildings such as shops, kitchens, restrooms and living spaces.

This was in contrast to Kuragala's setting, a scenic place with the aesthetics and atmosphere of an ancient forest cave monastery, offering views

Fig. 4.2 The Muslim 'Torana' beside the rock-cut steps to Kuragala

of the plains stretching to the borders of Monaragala District and the east coast beyond. The view of the ancient temple at Budugala, close to Kuragala, and the surrounding paddy fields is breathtaking. Hambantota to the south is visible and the new Mattala Airport. Kuragala contains features of a religious sanctuary of bygone era, still ideal for meditation, and its impact has long been attested with Bassett writing that:

> a hermit can find solitude indeed and food for contemplation in the unbroken ocean of trees spread out below him...Earthly considerations lose their importance before the uncomplicated immensity of the colossal landscape and the fatality of the sheer abyss. (1934: 54–55)

4.3   The Daftar Gilani

To reach the Daftar Gilani mosque complex, one has to traverse the plateau, ascend another rocky hill and descend into a valley. There, at the entrance to the valley, is a large concrete signboard erected by the DoA in 1972, with the following Sinhala, Tamil and English text: "Kuragala Archaeological Reserve. Remains of an Ancient Buddhist Monastery, circa 2 Century BC" (Fig. 4.3). The board does not mention the 'Daftar Gilani' or any other Muslim designation within the site. The reserve covers four acres and the signboard informs people that they are entering an ancient sacred Buddhist site.

When one goes down the steps into the valley, the first feature encountered is a Muslim tomb near the bottom. A second tomb is visible about 100 metres along the path to the mosque. They are the first of the five tombs within the site and appear to belong to a more recent period, as pilgrims, mystics or patrons were interred there once the Kuragala pilgrimage became popular among Sri Lankan Muslims in the second quarter of the twentieth century. To the visitor, the tombs give the impression that this ancient Buddhist archaeological site is Muslim and one could argue that this has occurred with little regard for the cultural heritage, history, archaeology or monuments of Kuragala.

The mosque itself is located on the rock outcrop close to a rock shelter to the south. This outcrop is called Hituvangala, or 'standing rock' in Sinhala, but in Tamil it is known as the Kappal Malai, or 'ship mountain'. To the south-west is a peak called Jin Malai, or 'spirit mountain' in Tamil, with a further five rock shelters widely believed to have been used for meditation by Buddhist monks as well as Sufi mystics. To the east is the peak with the Kuragala rock shelter, or in Tamil the Curankam Malai, or 'cave mountain', in which the Persian Sufi mystic Muhyiuddin

Fig. 4.3 The Department of Archaeology's signboard at Kuragala

Abdul Qadir al-Gilani spent time on his way to Sri Pada. It is alleged that this rock shelter contains a secret passageway to a building located in the plains far below.

The peak also hosts a half-built Buddhist *stupa* in an ancient style, which was repaired in the early 1970s by the DoA, leading to controversy. This historical site of Buddhist origin becomes vibrant annually during the Kanturi festival of the Sri Lankan and Indian Muslim community. The festival emerged to commemorate the death of Gilani and large crowds of Muslims gather at Kuragala and this tranquil location suddenly becomes full with pilgrims.

4.4   THE BURIED HISTORICITY OF KURAGALA

The 2013 remodelling was not the first recorded intervention at the site as there have been several earlier engagements between Muslim politicians, including Aboosally, Sinhala leaders, including the late President R. Premadasa (1924–1993) and concerned Buddhist monks and local lay people to reach conciliatory measures with regard to the use of the sacred site.

However, research of official British reports helps to contextualize the nature of the growth in Muslim pilgrimage to Kuragala. In contrast to earlier years, and after the 1915 Sinhala-Muslim riots, the *Ceylon Administration Report for 1919* (CAR) contains a lengthy section on pilgrimages in Sabaragamuva Province. After giving a detailed account of the most prominent to Sri Pada, the last three lines of report recorded new and emerging pilgrimage sites: "less important pilgrimages are the Kuragala Muhammadan Pilgrimage, Alutnuwara Dewale Perahera Festival, and Boltumbe Dewale Perahera Festival" (CAR 1919: I2). The *Report* then added a remark indicating the growing significance of those pilgrimages for people who live in the region, as well as outside it: "These, too, attract people from several parts of the Island" (ibid.).

In later years, the *CARs* described the Kuragala pilgrimage with different terminologies and qualifying adjectives. Under the heading of 'Pilgrimages', the 1922 CAR described the Kuragala pilgrimage as "minor" and qualifying the dominant religion of the pilgrims as Muslim: "There were other minor festivals at Alutnuwera, Boltumbe, and Kuragala in Meda Korale is frequented by Muhammadans" (CAR 1922: I3). We do not hear in these reports, or in most of the literature on Kuragala, whether the pilgrims were of a Sufi-oriented religious persuasion or whether they were predominantly followers of the Qadiriyyat order that can be traced to Baghdad and Tamil Nadu (Schomburg 2003). The 1923 CAR also included Kuragala under the theme of pilgrimage and stated: "There were other minor festivals at Alutnuwera, Boltumbe, and Kuragala (Muhammadan)" (CAR 1923: I2).

Having first discussed pilgrimage to Sri Pada and Maha Saman Dewale as usual, the 1927 CAR recorded a growing religious phenomenon in Sabaragamuva Province. In one brief sentence, it recorded Kuragala under the heading of pilgrimage but, unlike previous reports, qualified the "frequented" pilgrims by using the plural noun "Muslims" as opposed to previous citations of "Muhammadan" or "Muhammadans": "Kūragala in Meda Korale is frequented by Muslims" (CAR 1927: I5). This change in the British word choice of 'Muslim' instead of 'Muhammadan' may reflect recommendations from a new Government appointed committee in 1924. Writing in 1932, Collins stated: "Kūragala is a great place of Muslim pilgrimage, though other religionists also claim it" (1932: 168).

CARs published after Independence in 1948 focused more on history, archaeology, monuments, prehistoric civilization and the rediscovered Buddhist features of Kuragala found in the jungle as opposed to the British colonial reports which offered sketchy ethnographic and administrative details of the pilgrimage, numbers, geographical orientations and ethnicity of pilgrims. For example, after a field visit of the DoA to explore the monuments at Kuragala, the *Sri Lanka Administration Report* for 1968–1969 (SLAR) recorded in Sinhala (my translation): "This area that contains Brahmi inscriptions with drip-ledged caves has now turned into a mosque of Muslim devotees. There are modern constructions of several buildings at the site" (SLAR 1968–1969: G31).

This archaeological report does three important things; firstly, it highlights the historical, archaeological and religious value of the monuments and visible remains at Kuragala. Secondly, it notes encroachment, deliberate and illegal occupation and significant religious transformations, such as the construction of the mosque, above older layers of historical monuments by a later religious group whose use of the site, practices there, and lifestyles and beliefs are different from those who inhabited those places and areas in previous centuries. Finally, it illustrates the dangers that historical and archaeological monuments face when new constructions are built on the top of historical sites without proper planning, permissions and consultations, particularly where little systematic archaeology has been conducted and few reports and assessments are available.

4.5 Exploration and Conservation

Building on this earlier exploration, The *Register of Ancient Monuments* (RAM) published by the Ministry of Cultural Affairs, records three archaeological sites in the broader geographical area that we today identify as Kuragala (1972: 701–703). These are Galtanyaya (125/4; 54/2), Kuragala (26/4; 55/2) and Budugala (27/4; 56/2). The first two are located in the village of Thanjantenna and the last in the adjoining village of Budugala. Explaining the archaeological importance of the first, and hinting at the necessity of preservation of the site, the *Register* states:

> [T]he remains of an ancient monastery in an area of about 5 acres surrounded by a prakara [parapet] of stone … Balustrade stones, stone steps and other remains of ancient structures partly buried can be noticed at the site. The remains of an ancient dagoba [*stupa*] are also at the site. This site which is very close to the Kuragala and Budugala sites may have found one unit with other sites. (Ministry of Cultural Affairs 1972: 701)

From this observation, it is clear that what we take today narrowly as Kuragala cannot be isolated from its wider geographical, religious and archaeological contexts.

The *Register* described Kuragala in the following words: "On a craggy site…is the ancient Buddhist monastic site of Kuragala. At the site are several drip-ledged caves. Some of which contain Brahmi inscriptions of the second and first centuries BC. On one of the rock hummocks here are the remains of a brick built dagoba [*stupa*]" (ibid.: 702).

From the accounts of Galtanyaya and Kuragala, it is clear the remains of a brick *stupa* is a common feature of both. This fact is relevant as recent accusations have been levelled at the DoA by a number of observers, including Aboosally (2002), that it had begun to build a new *stupa* on "the rock hummocks". This, I would argue, is a misrepresentation of the situation. Rather, the DoA has undertaken the conservation of the existing remains of an ancient *stupa*. This interpretation is supported by the notice issued by the Archaeological Commissioner on 13 September 1972 stating:

> Kuragala Archaeological Conservation. The Archaeological Department in pursuance of its policy of conserving ancient monuments is taking steps to start conservation work on the ancient ruins at the above site situated within its Reserves. It is not the intention of the Department to construct a New Dagoba [*stupa*] here. The Muslims who have been using Kuragala as a place of worship will not be affected by this conservation work.

With reference to the adjoining site, Budugala, the *Register* stated: "At this site are the remains of some double platformed buildings. In a cave here is a Brahmi inscription. Inside a cave of little depth is an ancient lavatory. Steps have been provided on the rock to give access to the dagoba which was on a large boulder at the site" (Ministry of Cultural Affairs 1972: 703). The site at Budugala shares many historical, archaeological and religious features with Galtanyaya and Kuragala. These combined reports confirm that all three sites form an almost contiguous belt around the hill that we now loosely call Kuragala.

4.6   Contested History of Kuragala

Accounts of Muslim claims to the historical site of Kuragala arise from the last few years of the nineteenth century and the early twentieth century. Ignoring the presence of the early Brahmi inscriptions of the second century BCE at the Hiṭuvangala shelter, British officials affirmed Kuragala as a "Mohammedan shrine" in the government printed maps of 1901 and 1928, reinforcing Muslim claims to Kuragala. Continuing narratives of Muslim claims to Kuragala and the perception of Kuragala as a 'Mohammedan shrine' were significantly reinforced in 1922 after the 1915 Sinhala-Muslim Riots with the construction of a new mosque on the site of an ancient Buddhist rock shelter with Brahmi inscriptions.

In 1932 Collins noted a contestation among Muslims in Kuragala: "The two Caves are occupied by one Ali Mustan, an Indian Muslim, who came to the place several years, and now lives there as a guide and friend of pilgrims, though his right to do so is strenuously resisted by the Muslim authorities of Balan-goda (sic)" (1932: 167). He also referred to an early version of the current name—"Dastar Selani"—used by Muslims:

> The special place of pilgrimage now is on the second cliff known as Dastar Selani...There were no devotees in these caves when I was there, but it is not unusual for Muslim pilgrims...to stay here for three months...There was, however, one delightful gentleman from Lahore in one of the lower caves. (Ibid.: 168)

The mosque constructed at Hituvangala is now known among Muslims as the Daftar Gilanī (or Daftar Jilani, Daftar Jailani, Dafther Jailany). This identification, made in Hindi, Persian and Arabic, is used both for the mosque as well as for the wider sacred area. This usage for ancient Kuragala can be contested as a case of intentional 'Islamization' of the site and a deliberate attempt to 'replace' traditional Sinhala names. One could argue this is an indication of an 'intention to replace' the Buddhist origins of the site. It is not yet certain when Muslims first began to use the name 'Daftar Gilani' replacing the traditional name Kuragala.

Perhaps later than 1898 as, during British rule, the name 'Kooragala', a spelling variation, was used by the Government Agent in his letter to Muslims in Balangoda on 23 April 1898. What is certain is that neither the British officials in the nineteenth century, nor Muslims of Balangoda at that time, referred to the 'Daftar Gilani' or other versions of that name until the 1930s.

Muhyiuddin Abdul Qadir al-Gilani (1077–1166 CE) was a Sufi mystic born in Gilan, a town in the region of Persia near the Caspian Sea. Gilani carried out intensive study in the Islamic sciences for many years in Baghdad. It is said that Gilani left Baghdad to commit himself to pursuance of ascetic disciplines. In an extensive period of training, it is believed Gilani may have travelled to Sri Lanka and Tamil Nadu as was the case with some prominent Sufi mystics such as Ibn Battuta (Deegalle 2018)]. When he returned to Baghdad in his early forties, he took up further mystical training. Through teaching, preaching and administration, Gilani earned a reputation for great piety and mystical achievements and received the appellation of Muhyiuddin or 'Reviver of Islam'. He died and was buried in Baghdad and his children and disciples established the Qadiriyyat order (Schomburg 2003: 21).

There is an important popular narrative among Muslims that reinforces their claim to Kuragala, which records that Gilani spent 12 years meditating at the site (Aboosally 2002; McGilvray 2017: 274). There is no evidence to substantiate this claim; nevertheless, it suggests a historical precedence of Muslim right to the ancient site as a place of worship before the later nineteenth century resurgence of the site and the construction of the mosque at the shelter in 1922 (Aboosally 2002: 59; McGilvray 2017: 275).

The mosque at Kuragala became a locus of veneration for Gilani in the twentieth century. Referring to the mosque, and its close link with the Sufi mystic, Schomburg wrote:

> The Daftar Jailani site in the south-central highlands of Sri Lanka presents special features both because of its Sri Lankan location and because of its isolated mountain jungle situation. The saint [Gilani] is supposed to have rested and meditated here on his pilgrimage to Adam's Peak, the mountaintop site Muslims revere as the spot where Prophet Adam came to earth. Daftar Jailni ('Cave of Gilani') is so named because of the cliff-edge cave at this site, where the saint meditated; his barakat [spiritual energy] is attested by the miraculous light said to glimmer in the deep recesses of the cave. (2003: 28–29)

There were legal battles among Muslims concerning the affairs of the mosque as early as 1922 (Police Court Case No. 22494 of 1922). However, it was only in the late 1960s that Buddhists got involved significantly in religiously and politically motivated activities at the site, including a legal case in which the Government filed a lawsuit against a mendicant, Trinco Bawa, for constructing a building in defiance of the *Antiquities Ordinance* (Aboosally 2002: 84). The twenty-first century has witnessed increased tension on the issue of legitimacy of a Muslim group controlling the affairs of ancient Buddhist Kuragala. The *Bodu Bala Sena* and *Sinhala Ravaya* pressed the Rajapaksa Government to address the issue and resolve potential threats it may have for peace and harmony. As noted earlier, in response to this the Defense Secretary visited the site in April 2013 and ordered 'illegal' structures around the immediate vicinity of mosque, to be relocated (McGilvray 2016: 69).

4.7 Conclusion

This case study described the dangers facing Kuragala from rapid development and encroachment. There are similar threats to other monuments in Sri Lanka. While economic, political, ethnic and religious explanations for illegal intrusions may be provided, these actions damage heritage and present the risk of depriving the narration of an 'untold' story of a monument for future generations. Surely, new constructions on archaeological sites without proper assessments are unacceptable. It can be argued that relatively new constructions on the top of earlier sites can be revisited for excavation and can be shifted to different locations if they pose dangers by irreversibly damaging cultural heritage. It should also be recognized that this is not just the case of the more recent Muslim monuments built at Kuragala but can also be applied to the case of new Buddhist monuments above ancient Buddhist sites, such as those within 60 metres of the Sri Mahabodhi in Anuradhapura's UNESCO World Heritage Site.

This chapter has also examined how two contemporary Sri Lankan religious communities, Buddhist and Muslim, have been contesting each other's claim for the sacred ground at Kuragala on the basis of legends, memorials, archaeological monuments, inscriptions, colonial records and legal and historical documents. From the early twentieth century onwards, Kuragala has become an intensely disputed sacred site. In the imagination of cultural heritage of Buddhists the visible 'Islamization' of Kuragala, including renaming and building new constructions on an archaeological site has aroused strong emotions and been intensely questioned. This also has political ramifications and affects harmonious and functional relationships both locally and more widely in Sri Lanka. Legal issues, including the implementation of *The Antiquities Ordinance No. 9 of 1940* that regulates governance of archaeologically protected sites, have been used to remove illegally constructed recent buildings from the archaeological site. Religious and ethnic tensions that informed the contestation of the sacred space of Kuragala have been briefly touched upon with the intention of exploring them further in the future.

REFERENCES

Aboosally, M. L. M. (2002). *Dafther Jailany: A Historical Account of the Dafther Jailani Rock Cave Mosque*. Colombo: Sharm Aboosally.

Bassett, R. H. (1934). *Romantic Ceylon: Its History, Legend and Story*. Colombo: Ceylon Colombo Apothecaries.

Ceylon Administrative Reports (CAR): 1919, 1922, 1923 and 1927.

Collins, C. H. (1932). "The Archaeology of the Sabaragamuwa Bintenna." *Journal of the Royal Asiatic Society (Ceylon Branch)*, 32(85), 158–192.

Deegalle, M. (2004). "Politics of the Jathika Hela Urumaya Monks: Buddhism and Ethnicity in Contemporary Sri Lanka." *Contemporary Buddhism*, 5(2), 83–103.

Deegalle, M. (2018). "Sri Pada Sacred to Many: Sufi Mystics on Pilgrimage to Adam's Peak." In I. Yusuf (Ed.), *Multiculturalism in Asia: Peace and Harmony* (pp. 40–69). Bangkok: Mahidol University and Konrad Adenauer Stiftung.

McGilvray, D. B. (2016). "Islamic and Buddhist Impacts on the Shrine at Daftar Jailani, Sri Lanka." In D. Dandekar & T. Tschacher (Eds.), *Islam, Sufism and Everyday Politics of Belonging in South Asia* (pp. 62–76). London: Routledge.

McGilvray, D. B. (2017). "Jailani: A Sufi Shrine in Sri Lanka." In I. Ahmad & H. Helmut Reifeld (Eds.), *Lived Islam in South Asia* (pp. 273–289). London: Routledge.

Ministry of Cultural Affairs. (1972). *Register of Ancient Monuments*. Colombo: Ministry of Cultural Affairs.

Paranavitana, S. (1970). *Inscriptions of Ceylon: Volume 1*. Colombo: The Department of Archaeology.

Schomburg, S. E. (2003). *Reviving Religion: The Qadiri Sufi Order, Popular Devotion to Sufi Saint Muhyiuddin Abdul Qadir al-Gilani, and Processes of 'Islamization' in Tamil Nadu and Sri Lanka*. Ph.D. Dissertation, Unpublished Harvard University.

Somadeva, R., Wanninayaka, A., & Devage, D. (2015). *Kaltota Survey Phase I: Memoirs of the Postgraduate Institute of Archaeology No. 3*. Colombo: Postgraduate Institute of Archaeology.

Sri Lanka Administration Report (SLAR) for 1968–1969.

CHAPTER 5

Community Engagement in the Greater Lumbini Area of Nepal: The Micro-Heritage Case Study of Dohani

Nick Lewer, Anouk Lafortune-Bernard, Robin Coningham, Kosh Prasad Acharya and Ram Bahadur Kunwar

Abstract This chapter describes the historical and modern importance of the Greater Lumbini Area of Nepal from the perspective of its many large and small archaeological sites, and the importance of preserving and protecting its living cultural heritage. Issues include the impact of industrial infrastructure development and a corresponding increase in

N. Lewer (✉)
Coral Associates Ltd, North Yorkshire, UK
e-mail: nick.lewer@coralassociates.org

A. Lafortune-Bernard · R. Coningham
Durham University, Durham, UK
e-mail: anouk.lafortune-bernard@durham.ac.uk

R. Coningham
e-mail: r.a.e.coningham@durham.ac.uk

K. P. Acharya · R. B. Kunwar
Department of Archaeology, Government of Nepal, Kathmandu, Nepal

© The Author(s) 2019
R. Coningham and N. Lewer (eds.), *Archaeology, Cultural
Heritage Protection and Community Engagement in South Asia*,
https://doi.org/10.1007/978-981-13-6237-8_5

59

air pollution, the positive and negative impact and opportunities as a result from a rise in tourism (particularly pilgrims), encroachment, and the needs of community economic benefit. Using Dohani as a case study, the approaches and methodologies used for community consultation and engagement in heritage protection at a micro-heritage site are described and their effectiveness considered. Challenges for the community include those of motivation, sustainability, coordination between agencies, governance and the role of volunteers.

Keywords Nepal · Dohani · Community · Heritage protection

5.1   INTRODUCTION

This chapter focuses on the historical and modern importance of the Greater Lumbini Area (GLA)of Nepal within the context of its many archaeological sites and the importance of preserving and protecting its living cultural heritage. Issues include the impact of infrastructure development and the positive and negative impact and opportunities that arise from the rise in tourism, particularly pilgrims. Referencing Dohani as a case study, the approaches and methodologies used for community consultation and engagement in heritage protection at a micro-heritage site are described and their effectiveness considered particularly in relation to how communities living nearby may benefit socially, spiritually and economically from archaeological activities. We acknowledge the generosity of Durham University and Durham's UNESCO Chair in allowing this chapter to be made Open Access to reach and influence as wide an audience as possible.

5.2   THE GREATER LUMBINI AREA (GLA)

5.2.1   *Demographics*

The GLA, with its rich tangible and intangible Buddhist heritage, is located in Nepal's western Terai and stretches across the districts of Nawalparasi, Rupandehi and Kapilbastu. Recently incorporated into Nepal's new Federal Province No. 5, identity groups include indigenous peoples such as the Tharu communities and those who have migrated

Table 5.1 Overview of the population of the Greater Lumbini Area based on Nepal's 2011 National Population Census Data

	Rupandehi District (%)	Kapilbastu District (%)	Nawalparasi District (%)
Hindu	86	81	88
Muslim	8	18	4
Other	6	1	8

to the Terai over the last century, mainly from the hill regions of Nepal and from India (Whelpton 2005; Gaige 2009). The population is predominantly Hindu with a significant Muslim minority, but few Buddhists (Table 5.1).

Economic activity in the GLA is primarily agricultural but industry is developing along the highways and in cities, particularly in Rupandehi District (CBS 2014a). Kapilbastu is the least advanced of the three districts with numerous developmental challenges including weak governance, communal tensions between Hindu and Muslim communities as well as with recent internal migrant groups, flooding during the monsoon, and the prevalence of traditional practices of caste and gender-based discrimination (CBS 2012a, b; 2014a, b, c, d; UNDP and Government of Nepal 2014).

5.2.2   Buddhist Heritage

Rupandehi District is home to the garden of Lumbini, birthplace of the Buddha, which he identified as one of four sites that his disciples should visit on pilgrimage. The other three are in modern India: Bodh Gaya, where he found enlightenment; Sarnath, where he gave his first teaching; and Kusinagara, where he attained *parinirvana* or 'great passing away' (Weise 2013). Kapilbastu District has other important sites linked to early Buddhism, including Tilaurakot, thought to be ancient Kapilavastu, childhood home of the Buddha and capital city of his father Suddhodana. Sandstone pillars at Gotihawa and Niglihawa record early royal patronage and pilgrimage to Buddhist sites as they reference, as does the pillar at Lumbini, visits from the Emperor Asoka in the third century BCE (Coningham et al. 2015). The last of these major sites is

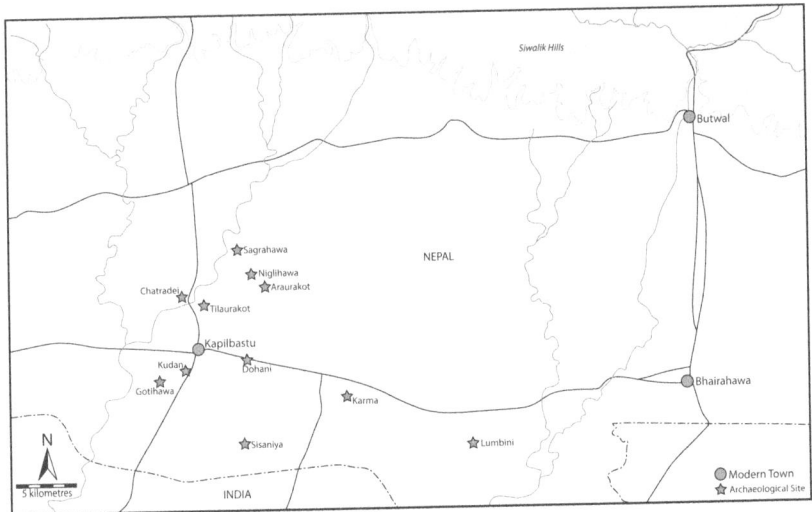

Fig. 5.1 Map of key heritage and archaeology sites within the Greater Lumbini Area

the stupa at Ramagrama in Nawalparasi District, believed to be one of the first *stupas* built after the Buddha's *parinirvana* and the only one that has remained unopened, thus containing an original share of his corporeal relics (Fig. 5.1).

These locations were identified in the late nineteenth century during explorations to rediscover Buddhist sites mentioned in historical and religious texts (Allen 2008; Coningham 2001; Führer 1972; Mukherji 1901). However, little research had been undertaken until the late 1960s when, with UN support, initiatives began to develop Lumbini as an international centre of pilgrimage and tourism (Joury 1969). The Lumbini Master Plan (LMP) was finalized in 1978 (Tange & URTEC 1978) and is being implemented by the Lumbini Development Trust (LDT). While Lumbini was included on UNESCO-'s World Heritage list in 1997, other Nepali sites remain at the edge of larger pilgrimage circuits, primarily centred around Lumbini and Indian centres such as Bodh Gaya, Rajgir, and Sarnath (Table 5.2). However, with the LMP reaching its final stage of implementation and visitor numbers expected to reach two million by 2020, there is interest in the development of other Nepali sites as part of the GLA's economic development.

Table 5.2 Annual visitor numbers at selected sites within the Buddhist circuits of north-east India and Nepal

Sites	Bodh Gaya[a]	Sarnath[b]	Rajgir[a]	Lumbini[c]	Tilaurakot[c]
Numbers	2,040,625	1,455,271	1,683,723	1,550,000	38,239

[a]Source Bihar Tourism Statistics 2018
[b]Source Uttar Pradesh Tourism Statistics 2018
[c]Source Lumbini Development Trust

5.2.3 Economic Development

The GLA's Buddhist archaeological heritage has been highlighted as a key development asset (UNFCO 2013: 11). As a result, the World Bank/International Finance Corporation and Asian Development Bank (ADB) are upgrading regional infrastructure, including road widening and transforming Bhairahawa airport into an international facility (ADB 2018a, b; IFC 2013). Their objectives also include the improvement of infrastructure at key heritage sites, the development of a promotional plan, and support for business initiatives (TRC 2013; ETG 2013; CTCA 2014). Interest from international Buddhist stakeholders has increased with, for example, the construction of new monasteries at Tilaurakot and Kudan in Kapilbastu District under the auspices of Lumbini's Royal Thai Monastery. However, visitor number growth, along with accelerated development in the GLA, has adversely affected the preservation of archaeological sites and impacted on local communities (Coningham et al. 2017). One unwelcome spin-off is an increase in environmental degradation and air pollution as industry has spread along upgraded road networks (Vivekanda 2017).

In 2013, an Integrated Management Plan (IMP) was prepared for Lumbini with the aims of redefining the management framework of Lumbini and planning future local and regional initiatives to ensure the sustainable development of the GLA. Other objectives included research and development of sites while prioritizing conservation and facilitating 'strategies for poverty alleviation of the local communities and to develop tourism and pilgrimage by means of improving facilities, services, infrastructure and accessibility of heritage sites' (Weise 2013: 7). The IMP proposed applying for World Heritage Site status for Tilaurakot and Ramagrama to provide more diversity for visitors and to promote the Terai as an important destination for cultural and religious tourism. Following the IMP's recommendations, the Japanese-Fund-in-Trust-for-UNESCO Project *Strengthening the Conservation and the Management of Lumbini, Birthplace of Lord Buddha, World Heritage Site, Phase 2 (2014–2017)*, under the overall leadership of Professor Yukio Nishimura of the University of Tokyo, began a programme of multi-disciplinary research in Kapilbastu District, with Tilaurakot as its main location, focused on three aspects: archaeological investigations, conservation, and design and planning (Coningham et al. 2017). An associated programme was also developed to start mapping the perceptions and use of archaeological and sacred sites by users and stakeholders, and how these may be impacted by excavations and other interventions (Lafortune-Bernard et al. 2018a, b). This data is being used to help understand the balance between the protection of ancient heritage with local communities and visitor needs. For example, in some places encroachment and soil extraction were degrading heritage, and this required consultation and participation of local communities to resolve. At Kudan, a fence had been built between the archaeological site and the local village in an effort to protect the site from cattle, but which separated the people from a shrine that was in daily use - an example of an 'outside' heritage protection initiative that introduced separations which did not exist previously between residents and their living heritage. Such observations emphasized the importance of strengthening community participation in site custodianship to ensure that connected communities benefit from, or at least are not harmed by, archaeological needs (Coningham et al. 2017).

5.3   Dohani

Dohani is located six kilometres south-east of Tilaurakot on the main Taulihawa-Lumbini road. In 2011 the population of Dohani was 6721 with 27 different caste, religious or ethnic groups and seven mother tongues spoken, mainly Awadhi and Urdu, with very few native Nepali speakers. In terms of identity, 30% were classified as lower caste; 20% Muslim; 20% Yadav; 15% Kurmi; and 15% others (CBS 2014b). Dohani's social capital is rich and includes CBOs and NGOs such as women's micro-credit groups, a child rights group, Siddhartha Community Development which promotes children's education, a youth cricket club; Dalit

Association; Farmer's Cooperative; Mothers' Group; Ward Citizen Forum; Citizen Awareness Centre; and the Poverty Alleviation Cooperative. It has four government schools, four private schools and four madrasas.

The main livelihood is derived from agriculture, with some employment in public service, businesses such as a rice mill, teashops and food shops, sewing, pottery, fish farms and rice-frying. Most people own their homes and have land that is used for domestic vegetable and crop production. The main road through Dohani has been widened to improve connections between Lumbini and Kapilbastu District, especially Taulihawa and Tilaurakot. With envisaged increases in visitor numbers, there is the potential for Dohani to become an attraction for pilgrims travelling between Lumbini and Tilaurakot.

The archaeological site of Dohani is demarcated by a fence with a boundary of about 1.5 kilometres and comprises uncultivated land containing a broad low mound, threshing areas, haystacks and has cattle grazing on it. Within the site, there is a local shrine dedicated to the goddess Samai Mai. Archaeological investigations started in 2015 when a team from the Japanese-Funds-in-Trust-for-UNESCO project and the Department of Archaeology (DoA) completed a geophysical survey and identified a small square clay fortification with rounded towers at each corner (Fig. 5.2). The DoA then excavated in 2017 and 2018,

Fig. 5.2 Plan of the archaeological site of Dohani with geophysical survey overlay

exposing part of the eastern fortification wall. Evidence of early occupation dating back to the first millennium BCE was recovered, followed by the later establishment of the small fort during the Kushana Period (100 BCE–300 CE). Dohani's location, and that of a similarly shaped monument at Karma, suggests that it functioned as a waystation for people moving along the old pilgrim road between Lumbini and settlements to its west.

5.4   DOHANI COMMUNITY CONSULTATION AND ENGAGEMENT

5.4.1   *Purpose and Methodology*

The key objectives of consultation are to carry out discussions with communities to explore ways in which people can be collaboratively involved in the protection of an archaeological site, and to discuss the future development of tourism and pilgrimage so that local people may benefit economically while protecting their own cultural heritage and social values.

Before the community consultation at Dohani began, a survey team was constituted with the LDT, DoA officers and volunteers from local schools and administrations, and a training programme was organized to prepare them for community interviews. This consisted of site visits to Dohani and Kapilvastu, when the significance of the sites was explained, a questionnaire was reviewed and refined, and processes for working in small teams discussed. Six interview teams with three people in each were formed.

The methodology used at Dohani employed individual and household interviews using a questionnaire that allowed for open and closed questions, and with space for discussion; focus groups with women, youth and men; key informant interviews; and random 'informal' meetings. Questions explored a range of issues asking, for example, about any history of illegal soil quarrying close to site boundaries; encroachment; land ownership; economic and trading factors related to development; peoples knowledge of the site; community development needs (education, economic, infrastructure etc.) in relation to future archaeology excavations and potential pilgrimage activity; usage of site by people; existing craft manufacture; markets; and skill availability. Follow-up visits and meetings were held to monitor and discuss changes in community engagement as a result of these consultations.

5.4.2   *Community Consultation Findings*

Interviews at Dohani indicated that:

- People knew little about the site except for the Samai Mai shrine and its use for occasional social gatherings. Samai Mai is a powerful goddess who villagers worship regularly but the biggest festival occurs during the poya full moon at Vesak when people who have had their wishes fulfilled go to the shrine to give offerings. People also walked around the shrine in the event of smallpox outbreaks. If the elephants get broken, the village repairs it. There is also a tradition for newly married couples to visit Samai Mai. The current shrine on the archaeological mound was built by a Saddhu 15 years ago but has a longer history. The Saddhu has since died but his brother and nephew still care for it.
- The site was used for livestock grazing, threshing, hay storage and as a toilet for some nearby houses.
- It received few visitors from outside Dohani.
- People were curious to learn more.
- The land demarcated by DoA markers was generally respected (Lewer and Lafortune-Bernard 2017).

The community consultation was used to identify potential partners with whom archaeologists could develop a programme to engage residents with the site development and protection. Teachers from schools in Dohani were very helpful and discussions with them highlighted constraints and opportunities to their engagement in helping with the care of the site:

- They had little knowledge about the local heritage and ancient history of the region, particularly early Buddhism;
- There was a lack of educational material for teaching school children about the heritage and the history of the region;
- It was difficult to organize site visits to nearby archaeological sites, like Tilaurakot and Kudan, due to limited funds and transportation costs. Another problem was availability of a knowledgeable guide to provide information about the sites;
- The presence of archaeologists at the site was seen as an opportunity to start designing activities for the schools and local community.

5.4.3 Community Engagement

5.4.3.1 First Excavation Season (Jan–Feb 2017)

A meeting was organized at which teachers, DoA officers, and a facilitator from Durham's UNESCO Chair attended. The main outcome was that participants agreed to form a Community Group with the objectives of helping protect Dohani and raising awareness about local heritage. A series of actions were identified for each partner to support the creation of the Group and its activities, and a Committee was formed to write a constitution. This meant that the Group could be registered with the District Office thus giving access to funding sources. The Durham facilitator and DoA officers agreed to write a booklet on the archaeological heritage of the region as a teaching resource and also a leaflet on the archaeological site, to be finalized in collaboration with the Committee at the following excavation season (January–February 2018). DoA officers gave a site tour to all participants providing information on the site and the latest findings. Follow-up meetings were organized to support the Committee in preparing District Office registration and to discuss the organization of a joint event to mark the end of the archaeological field season in Dohani. The Committee also organized an event for the site visit of the Japanese-Funds-In-Trust-for-UNESCO International Scientific Committee at which the archaeologists had prepared a temporary exhibition of excavated artefacts.

5.4.3.2 Second Excavation Season (Jan–Feb 2018)

The Committee reported that there was difficulty with the process of registering the Group with the District Office due in part to the restructuring of regional and local administrations in Nepal as a result of the process of Federalization (Accord 2017). It was decided to invite the newly elected Ward Chair to become Patron of the Committee and to ask the new Ward to become a partner and to provide support to the teachers in their interaction with the appropriate government offices. Governance restructuring integrated Dohani within Kapilavastu Municipality and it was agreed necessary to assess the potential interest of Municipal offices, local CBOs and NGOs to support the activities of the Committee.

As well as actions taken to establish more permanent structures and resources for the Committee, progress was made in developing educational material for dissemination by teachers. A first version of the booklet and leaflet were finalized with the Committee and are currently (June 2018) being tested for one year at Dohani schools and, drawing from teachers' feedback, these will be revised during the next field season (January 2019). The DoA arranged a site visit for staff and school students from Dohani to further stimulate awareness and interest. The President of the Dohani Committee was involved in the organization of the 'Tilaurakot Heritage Festival', an event jointly organized by Durham's UNESCO Chair, the LDT and DoA in collaboration with an Organising Committee composed of local teachers and Kapilavastu Municipality's Education Officer. At the festival, Dohani school students participated in drawing and speech competitions.

5.5   Conclusion

New micro-heritage sites like Dohani, that are overshadowed by macro-heritage destinations such as Lumbini and Tilaurakot, present particular challenges. Persuading local communities to engage in heritage protection is difficult when there is initially little evidence of a more permanent visitor attraction and there is no immediate benefit economically. Dohani is a majority Hindu community with little recent Buddhist heritage, so there is a social and spiritual disconnect with the ancient Buddhist pilgrimage history, and the community associates more with the Samai Mai shrine and this is their more powerful contemporary and experiential focus. As excavations proceed, and uncovering more of the site's heritage, it will be interesting to see if such discoveries affect people's view of their identity and connections with the wider society (Fig. 5.3).

As we noted in the Introduction to this book, community-led processes take time and require a long-term commitment of support so that they develop in depth. Providing consistent and sustainable support to the Dohani Committee was problematic. Bursts of activity happened during the fieldwork phases and this stimulated people's interest and allowed contact with archaeologists, but after the site had been closed and the excavation team departed interests waned. Protection at micro-heritage sites may rely on volunteers and it is important to look at what motivates people to take on an unpaid role as it might be that they see business, social and/or spiritual benefits. DoA personnel had sporadic contact with the Dohani Committee between excavations and a Facebook Page was established which provided news and photographs.

Fig. 5.3 Samai Mai Shrine at Dohani archaeological site

What is also clear is that the integration of the different levels of governance (local, regional, national, international) is needed to ensure that there is complementarity of actions between archaeological excavations and protection measures with the wider economic and development infrastructure plans. This means regular consultation between the local community, business and tourism sectors perhaps designing an integrated framework for these factors. The DoA is particularly well placed to take the role of lead coordination agency for this.

We agree with Weerasinghe (2017) that heritage value lies in a combination of the archaeological, the natural and the traditional. Collaborating with individuals and organizations specializing in understanding community social capital and social fabric to undertake a more in-depth study of the Dohani community is needed to properly realize these connections. To give credibility to community engagement's claim of putting people at the centre, more effective ways are being explored of bringing Dohani's community into archaeological project conceptualization and management, 'academic' platforms, and dissemination conferences so that their voice is meaningfully heard and listened to. This was, of course, a pilot study but a critical one, to experiment with balancing the needs of macro-heritage sites with potential for enhancing smaller, less prestigious micro-heritage sites and investigate the potential of twin-tracks for sustainable heritage development. Longitudinal mapping and engagement will allow us to evaluate the success of this pilot and its transferability to similar contexts.

REFERENCES

Accord. (2017). *Two Steps Forward, One Step Back: The Nepal Peace Process.* London: Conciliation Resources.

ADB. (2018a). *South Asia Tourism Infrastructure Development Project (Bangladesh, India, and Nepal): Project Data Sheet.* https://www.adb.org/projects/39399-013/main#project-pds.

ADB. (2018b). *SASEC Tourism Development Project: Project Data Sheet.* https://www.adb.org/projects/39399-012/main#project-pds.

Allen, C. (2008). *The Buddha and Dr Führer: An Archaeological Scandal.* London: Haus Publishing.

Bihar Tourism. (2018). *Statistics of Domestic and Foreign Tourists Visit to the State of Bihar (Year-2017 January to December).* http://www.bihartourism.gov.in/data/Tourist_Data/Monthly%20Staticts%20of%20Dom%20and%20for%20final-2017.pdf.

CBS. (2012a). *National Population and Housing Census 2011 (Village Development Committee/ Municipality)*. Kathmandu, Nepal: Central Bureau of Statistics.

CBS. (2012b). *National Population and Housing Census 2011 (National Report)*. Kathmandu: Central Bureau of Statistics.

CBS. (2014a). *National Population and Housing Census 2011 (Village Development Committee/Municipality) Rupandehi*. Kathmandu: Central Bureau of Statistics.

CBS. (2014b). *National Population and Housing Census 2011 (Village Development Committee/Municipality) Kapilbastu*. Kathmandu: Central Bureau of Statistics.

CBS. (2014c). *National Population and Housing Census 2011, Volume 5, Part XI: Economic Characteristics Tables*. Kathmandu: Central Bureau of Statistics.

CBS. (2014d). *National Population and Housing Census 2011, Volume 5, Part III: Social Characteristics Tables (Disability, Literacy Status and Educational Attainment)*. Kathmandu: Central Bureau of Statistics.

Coningham, R. A. E. (2001). The Archaeology of Buddhism. In T. Insoll (Ed.), *Archaeology and World Religion* (pp. 61–95). London: Routledge.

Coningham, R. A. E., Acharya, K. P., Kunwar, R. B., Manuel, M. J., Davis, C. E., & Lafortune-Bernard, A. (2017). Promoting the Protection, Preservation and Presentation of the Natal Landscape of the Buddha in Nepal. In P. Gunawardhana, R. A. E. Coningham, & K. Nampoothiri (Eds.), *Buddha Rashmi Vesak* (Vol. 2017, pp. 13–26). Colombo: Central Cultural Fund.

Coningham, R. A. E., Acharya, K. P., & Manuel, M. (2014). *Strengthening the Conservation and Management of Lumbini, the Birthplace of the Lord Buddha, World Heritage Property (Phase II): Final Report of the First Season*. Unpublished UNESCO Report.

Coningham, R. A. E., Acharya, K. P., & Manuel, M. (2015). *Strengthening the Conservation and Management of Lumbini, the Birthplace of the Lord Buddha, World Heritage Property (Phase II): Final Report of the Second Season*. Unpublished UNESCO Report.

CTCA. (2014). *Tourism Promotion Plan for Lumbini and Adjoining Areas: Towards Making the Buddha's Birth Places & Associated Sites a Regional Tourism Hub (2015–2024)*. Kathmandu: Ministry of Culture, Tourism and Civil Aviation.

ETG. (2013). *Greater Lumbini Tourism Cluster Competitiveness Strategy*. Unpublished report for the World Bank.

Führer, A. (1972 reprint of 1889). *Antiquities of Buddha Sakyamuni's Birthplace in the Nepalese Tarai*. Varanasi: Indological Book House.

Gaige, F. H. (2009). *Regionalism and National Unity in Nepal*. Lalitpur: Himal Book.

IFC. (2013). *Investing in The Buddhist Circuit 2014–2018: Enhancing the Spiritual, Environmental, Social and Economic Value of the Places Visited by the Buddha in Bihar and Uttar Pradesh, India*. https://www.ifc. org/wps/wcm/connect/a0b004004618b490804eb99916182e35/ Buddhist+Circuit+Tourism+Strategy+Final.pdf?MOD=AJPERES.

Joury, Y. J. (1969). *A Brief on the Lumbini Development Project, April 1969*. Kathmandu: UN Resident Representative Office.

Lafortune-Bernard, A., Coningham, R. A. E., Acharya, K. P., & Kunwar, R. B. (2018a). Benchmarking the Social and Economic Impact of Pilgrimage at the site of Tilaurakot-Kapilvastu (Nepal). In P. Gunawardhana & R. Coningham (Eds.), *Buddha Rashmi Vesak Volume 2018*. Colombo: Central Cultural Fund: 85–96.

Lafortune-Bernard, A., Coningham, R. A. E., & Acharya, K. P. (2018b). Recording the Social and Economic Contribution of Local Heritage at Tilaurakot: A Pilot Study. In Oriental Cultural Heritage Sites Protection Alliance & M. Richon (Eds.), *The Cultural Heritage of Nepal, Before, During and After the 2015 Earthquakes: Current and Future Challenges*. Kathmandu: Vajra Books and Oriental Cultural Heritage Sites Protection Alliance.

Lewer, N., & Lafortune-Bernard, A. (2017). *Dohani Community Consultation 13 th–16th January 2017*. Coral Associates and Durham UNESCO Chair Unpublished Report.

Mukherji, P. C. (1901). *A Report on a Tour of Exploration of the Antiquities of Kapilavastu Tarai of Nepal During February and March 1899*. Calcutta: Office of the Superintendent of Government Printing.

Tange, K., & URTEC. (1978). *Master Design for the Development of Lumbini, Phase II. Final Report*. New York: UN.

TRC. (2013). *Tourism Cluster Analysis for Nepal Competitive Industries Diagnostic: Cluster Diagnostic Notes: Greater Lumbini & Palpa and Manaslu & Gorkha Clusters. Volume 1: Analysis*. Unpublished Report for the World Bank.

UNDP and Government of Nepal. (2014). *Nepal Human Development Report 2014: Beyond Geography Unlocking Human Potential*. http://www.hdr.undp. org/sites/default/files/nepal_nhdr_2014-final.pdf.

UNFCO. (2013). *District Profile: Kapilavastu, Nepal*. http://www.un.org.np/ sites/default/files/kapilvastu_district_profile.pdf.

Uttar Pradesh Tourism. (2018). *Annual Tourist Visits Statistics 2013–2017*.http://uptourism.gov.in/pages/top/about-up-tourism/ yearwise-tourist-stats.

Vivekanda, B. (2017). *Environmental Issues and Protection in Lumbini*. Conference Presentation at Pathways to the Protection and Rehabilitation of Cultural Heritage in South Asia, Kathmandu, September 2017.

Whelpton, J. (2005). *A History of Nepal*. Cambridge: Cambridge University Press.

Weerasinghe, J. (2017). *Sigiriya World Heritage Site. Global Heritage Commodified and Local Heritage Forgotten*. Conference Presentation at Pathways to the Protection and Rehabilitation of Cultural Heritage in South Asia, Kathmandu, September 2017.

Weise, K. (2013). *Strengthening Conservation and Management of Lumbini, the Birthplace of Lord Buddha, World Heritage Property: Integrated Management Framework*. Kathmandu: UNESCO.

CHAPTER 6

Protecting Heritage and Strengthening Community Engagement in Nepal

Marielle Richon

Abstract Richon describes the objectives of Oriental Cultural Heritage Sites Protection Alliance (the Alliance), a non-government not-for-profit organization to preserve and safeguard cultural heritage in Asia, and then focuses on its projects implemented in Nepal since 2013. Richon has worked with the Lopa community in the Medieval earthen walled city of Lo Manthang, which is on the Tentative List of Nepal for future World Heritage nomination, to harmonize relations between the community and Nepali authorities through a number of projects. Despite the 2015 Gorkha Earthquakes, the Alliance has completed a number of missions, workshops and publications. Richon argues that governments cannot be successful in managing national heritage without the support of local communities acting as stewards who understand and value its significance.

Keywords Nepal · Lo Manthang · Community · Heritage

M. Richon (✉)
International Council on Monuments and Sites (ICOMOS),
Paris, France
e-mail: marielrichon@orange.fr

© The Author(s) 2019
R. Coningham and N. Lewer (eds.), *Archaeology, Cultural Heritage Protection and Community Engagement in South Asia*,
https://doi.org/10.1007/978-981-13-6237-8_6

6.1   INTRODUCTION

Recognizing the significance and vulnerability of the cultural heritage of communities in Nepal, such as at the Birthplace of Lord Buddha at Lumbini, the Itum Baha Monastery in Kathmandu and the Medieval earthen walled city of Lo Manthang in Upper Mustang, the Oriental Cultural Heritage Sites Protection Alliance (the Alliance) initiated a series of preservation projects in 2013. From the beginning, the Alliance has respected the legitimate interests and concerns of all stakeholders, including the Government of Nepal, through its Department of Archaeology (DoA) as well as local communities.

In the Upper Mustang region of Nepal, the Lopa community of Lo Manthang was at first reluctant accepting outside interventions and interference with its environment and culture. Therefore, the Alliance's first actions were aimed at understanding the local context in all its dimensions: political, economic, environmental, religious, social, cultural and psychological. This resulted in a co-designed project aiming at harmonizing relations between all stakeholders. The shared objectives of this project are the preservation of the local tangible and intangible cultural heritage.

The 2015 Gorkha Earthquakes affected the Lopa community and generated a strong awareness among stakeholders about the need to rapidly undertake preservation interventions in order to protect local cultural heritage for future generations. This chapter will explore the manner in which the Alliance has contributed to building harmony between all stakeholders.

6.2   THE ORIENTAL CULTURAL HERITAGE
SITES PROTECTION ALLIANCE

The Alliance, also known as the Alliance de Protection du Patrimoine Culturel Asiatique, is a non-government organisation established in 2008 in Paris. A not-for-profit organization, its objective is to contribute to the protection of Asian cultural heritage by providing support for all forms of cooperation, particularly in the areas of safeguarding historical and cultural sites, in the context of urban economic and socio-cultural development, and also academic and research exchanges. It is committed to raising awareness in issues relating to Asian cultural heritage, and to promote exchanges, meetings and consultations that involve and engage particularly European and Asian experts, academics and others at the national and international levels. As such, the Alliance adheres to its mission for the conservation and promotion of key oriental cultural heritage sites by:

- facilitating cooperation between regions protecting historical and cultural relics, with the purpose of promoting urban economic and social development and of enhancing the communication and research between international experts in protecting cultural relics with the vast array of cultural professionals;
- drawing experts, universities and eminences both within and outside of the Alliance's attention to relevant issues concerning the conservation of oriental cultural heritage;
- promoting communications and negotiations between countries and nationalities over the issues of the conservation of cultural heritage as well as advancing contacts between universities and cultural industry professionals all around the world, especially Asian-Euro relationships;
- editing publications, works and literatures relevant to the conservation of oriental cultural heritage;
- organizing and participating in relevant researches and investigations as well as organizing working groups and to declaring recommendations or suggestions;
- organizing conferences, academic forums, academic first-hand investigations and explorations or to establish a platform for the expression of diversified academic opinions;
- cooperating with relevant European and Asian official persons in charge and technicians and mobilizing all the supporting forces as far-ranging as possible in order to create and develop an environment of active communication of experiences in terms of techniques, forms and facilities,
- guiding enterprises, foundations and media participation, and seeking to discuss with them events in which they have interest in order that relatively high symbolic values and substantial interactive signification can be manifested in their collaborations with the Alliance.

The Alliance has worked with the following partners to carry projects and conferences: the World Heritage Centre of UNESCO; UNESCO Kathmandu Office in Nepal; UNESCO New Delhi Office; UNESCO

Jakarta Office; DoA, Government of Nepal; Lumbini Development Trust (LDT); Kathmandu Valley Preservation Trust (KVPT); Department of Culture, Bhutan; Bureau of Cultural Heritage in the Taiwanese Ministry of Culture; Taipei National University of the Arts in Taiwan; Tainan National University of the Arts in Taiwan; Tianjin University in China; Durham University in the UK; Institute of Language and Culture Studies (ILCS), Royal University of Bhutan; University Paris IV Sorbonne; Ecole d'Architecture Paris La Villette; HimalAsia Foundation; Annapurna Conservation and Preservation Trust (ACAP); Kathmandu University; Lumbini Buddhist University; Tribhuvan University's Department of Architecture; Khwopa Engineering College; and ATELAB Laboratory, France.

6.3   THE ALLIANCE'S ACTIVITIES IN NEPAL

Since 2013 the Alliance has initiated and completed several projects in Nepal, notably in Lumbini, a UNESCO World Heritage property, and its surrounding Terai Region; in the Valley of Kathmandu, also a World Heritage property: and within the Medieval earthen walled city of Lo Manthang in Upper Mustang, which was inscribed on the Tentative List of Nepal in 2008 for a future nomination for World Heritage inscription. At Lumbini, the Alliance has supported a number of projects designed to engage with the World Heritage Site's local communities in order for them to improve their living conditions. Key to this transformation is the need to develop the region through cultural tourism and the creation of tourist itineraries out from Lumbini to its surroundings like Ramagrama, Tilaurakot, Kapilavastu - the ancient capital of the Sakya Kingdom and other significant sites. Recent UNESCO-sponsored archaeological campaigns have provided key evidence which highlights the important potential for future tourism development and, as discussed by Choegyal (see Chapter 7), the key driver is to encourage tourists and pilgrims to stay longer in the Terai region and discover other sites relating with the history of Lord Buddha's life and Buddhism. In order to create and start promoting these itineraries, the Alliance has sponsored a number of actions to reinforce the local community's capacities. These have consisted of training guides from the local resident communities at Tilaurakot through a new programme with experts. Earlier visitors had to rely on outside guides who had little up to date knowledge about the site. The Alliance has also reinforced capacity of infrastructure within the site of Tilaurakot by commissioning new signage and interpretation panels to enhance visitor experience, in partnership with

Durham University and UNESCO's Field Office in Nepal. The Alliance also supported the conception and publication of a tourist leaflet on Tilaurakot and Kapilavastu in partnership with the Lumbini Development Trust, Durham University and UNESCO's Field Office in Nepal.

The Alliance has also been active within the Kathmandu Valley, where it has supported the restoration of the thirteenth century CE Itum Baha Monastery, in partnership with KVPT. Believed to be one of the oldest Buddhist monasteries to survive within the Valley (Slusser 1982: 180), the complex comprises a central shrine in open rectangular courtyard formed by a quadrangle hosting residential and sacred functions (Andolfatto 2012: 77). The Itum Baha was severely damaged due to neglect as well as past and recent earthquakes but, with the help of the two Buddhist communities who share this monastery, Nepali carpenters and masons reinforced the existing structures and restored the damaged ones. A leaflet about the history and significance of this monastery is being co-designed in association with the leaders of the local communities and will be distributed with the entrance tickets sold to tourists. The benefits from sales to tourists will help improve the small free dispensary located inside the monastery premises. In the future, there are plans for a small site museum to be created in the attic in order to attract tourists, describe the restoration process and explain the significance of the monument. Information campaigns will also be organized in order for local guides to be aware of this restoration and include Itum Baha in their tours of the Valley of Kathmandu.

Following the severe impact on Kathmandu Valley after the 2015 Gorkha earthquake of 25th April, and aftershock of 12th May, the Alliance supported the rescue operations by sponsoring two young French architects and one French archaeology Ph.D. student to work for the UNESCO Field Office in Nepal for several months. This consisted of assisting Nepali authorities to document damaged monuments, securing the storage of architectural elements and artefacts, and in advising on the methodology for future restoration and reconstruction of major monuments. In 2018, the Alliance published *The Cultural Heritage of Nepal: Before, During and After the 2015 Earthquakes: Current and Future Challenges* (Oriental Cultural Heritage Sites Protection Alliance and Richon 2018: ISBN 9789937032032). The book contains chapters from 20 academics and experts from seven nationalities who analyse past and recent earthquakes effects and the way to anticipate them in order to protect the living cultural heritage of Nepal. It also emphasizes the cyclical nature of Nepali community resilience throughout its history as it hosts its living intangible heritage. Published through the Alliance, all profits generated by the sale of this publication will contribute to the safeguarding and restoration of the cultural heritage of Nepal.

6.4   Approaching Upper Mustang

Upper Mustang is a singular territory, which was closed by the Nepali Government for thirty years from 1962 (Tucci 1977; Peissel 1979). For this reason, basic infrastructure is still lacking; a gravel road was opened only in 2015, there is no hospital, and schools do not teach beyond eighth grade. The local Lopa community deplores this situation and is hostile towards the central authorities as it has the feeling that it is ignored and treated as second class citizenry. As a result, establishing trust was a major objective for the Alliance, ever since the Medieval earthen walled city of Lo Manthang was inscribed in 2008 by the Nepali Government on the Tentative List of Nepal for future World Heritage nomination (Selter 2007) (Fig. 6.1). The local community is broadly opposed to the idea of a potential inscription on the World Heritage List as it thinks that this inscription would be too prescriptive and prevent any change and development in and around the city. The Alliance's strategy to help build trust among the Nepali stakeholders is slow but long-term driven. It consists in raising the awareness of the local community through a series of meetings and in reinforcing the local capacities through training and capacity-building activities.

The Alliance initiated the organization of an International Symposium on 'Safeguarding Lo Manthang and the Cultural Landscape of Upper Mustang' between 1st and 2nd November 2013 in Kathmandu, in partnership with the DoA, HimalAsia Foundation, Kathmandu University and UNESCO Office in Nepal. During this Symposium, the results of the first phase of the comparative analysis of Lo Manthang were presented and several speakers expressed contrary views about a potential nomination of the Medieval earthen walled city of Lo Manthang for World Heritage inscription.

As a result, a fact-finding mission to Upper Mustang was organized by HimalAsia and Alliance between April and May 2014 with the participation of international experts from France, Germany and India. Students from Lumbini Buddhist University in Kathmandu and young Lopa students also participated. Working with the local associations of youth and

Fig. 6.1 Medieval city of Lo Manthang with its earthen wall

women, as well as with the Annapurna Conservation and Preservation Trust (ACAP), allowed participants to understand the context of Upper Mustang and its cultural and natural uniqueness. It was also an opportunity to reflect on the rapid cultural changes in Lo Manthang which were transforming local building techniques. This is particularly striking as building outside the medieval earthen wall was prohibited in the past but when the King of Mustang stepped down this became possible. Since 1992, some 27 doors or passages have been cut through the city's medieval earthen wall, fragilizing it dangerously. Getting to know the various stakeholders of the fortified city and the way decisions were made was important for co-designing future work.

In November 2014, the Alliance organized in Patan, Kathmandu, in partnership with KVPT, a one-week workshop on 'Architectural, Urban and Landscape Heritage of Lo Manthang and Upper Mustang: Conciliating Architectural Tradition and Modernity'. Participants included 19 students from Lumbini Buddhist University, Tribhuvan

University's Department of Architecture and Khwopa Engineering College in Nepal as well as six young Lopa. During the workshop, field visits to 10 Patan traditional houses transformed into tourist guesthouses were organized. Students were able to meet their owners and document the cost of transformation, issues met and solutions found through the use of traditional materials. The benefits of traditional materials in terms of economy, sustainability and tourist attractiveness in a seismic prone zone were explained. Participants also visited Bhaktapur, Vajrayogini and the early settlement of Sankhu, inscribed in 2008 on the Tentative List of Nepal for World Heritage nomination, within the Valley of Kathmandu. In addition to the visits to restored houses, the workshop included the co-design, elaboration and presentation of four micro-projects for Lo Manthang, each designed by one team. The definition of these micro-projects was co-designed by the four Lopa students who were distributed one to each team. The four topics were: traditional medicine, intangible cultural heritage, museum inventory and interpretation; parking for tourist vehicles away from the walled city; tourist homestay at traditional houses in Lo Manthang; preservation and modernization of traditional houses in Lo Manthang using traditional materials.

The first project aimed at preserving traditional medicine and intangible cultural heritage through a museum inventory and interpretation. This project focused on safeguarding the intangible cultural heritage of the Lopa community as a long-term theme. The team decided to start this twofold project by reorganizing the existing museum at Choede Monastery in Lo Manthang. The design proposed reorganizing the existing museum space by implementing modern museology (signage and interpretation), training monks to guide visitors in the museum in Nepali and English and creating an inventory and catalogue of artefacts that would be brought by the community to the Monastery in the future. To achieve this, it was recognized that the project needs to purchase a camera to create the catalogue but that the further development of side-objects for sale, such as postcards, calendars and flyers, would profit the Monastery and community. It was also agreed that, in the long-term, a craftsman could produce masks in front of visitors and thus create visibility and pride for living heritage, which would again benefit the community. To promote traditional Tibetan medicine, another proposal suggested organized visits to the Tibetan school in Lo Manthang for visitors to learn more about their practices. The subsequent sale of local medicinal plants and herbs, like herbal teas, would provide financial benefit to the school.

The second micro-project consisted in the creation of a car park away from the fortified sacred wall, known as the 'Chagri', as the local community has witnessed an increase in traffic and worries about the visual impact of trucks and jeeps on Lo Manthang (Fig. 6.2). The vibrations from some vehicles have damaged the structure of the wall and, in some places, generated collapses. The creation of a parking space away from the wall, well integrated in the landscape, would allow the local community to obtain some profit from the management of the parking for its own benefit and strengthen the capacity of Lo Manthang to preserve its cultural heritage thus bringing visibility, pride and tourism-related jobs.

The third micro-project focused on tourist homestays at Lo Manthang as homestays have been created successfully in other parts of Nepal (see Chapter 9). The aim was to create a pilot project to prove that homestay can work in Lo Manthang and convince some Lopa

Fig. 6.2 Abandoned truck next to chortens (*stupas*) outside Lo Manthang

families to take this initiative. The objective was to meet visitors, share the local lifestyle with them and increase family income while not disturbing the families' lifestyle. This project involved the selection of a pilot home among the Lopa community, investigate the legal aspects of homestays, document successful homestays in other regions of Nepal, train a host-family to welcoming visitors (food, hygiene, etc.), determine which rooms in the selected home should be dedicated to visitors, address issues including hygiene, toilets and showers, as well as medical concerns such as altitude, food and water for visitors.

The fourth, and last, micro-project concerned the preservation of the traditional built heritage of Lo Manthang, with a focus on the careful analysis of the causes of the deterioration of Lo Manthang's built heritage, namely neglect, leakage, loss of know-how in masonry and carpentry and modern materials being preferred to traditional ones. The objectives of this project were multifold as it aimed to motivate the local community to use traditional building techniques and materials by involving local masons and carpenters, lifting misconceptions about modern materials and raising awareness of the pertinence of local materials' features and qualities, fighting water seepage through roofs and leakage through walls. It was hoped that the implementation of this project would result in using a mix of traditional and modern materials such as 'pang' made of mud and vegetation, bentonite clay or 'Tsharangkeisa' and polyethylene sheets, inventorying and mapping leakages in Lo Manthang, testing, building prototypes, documenting the best solutions and working in the longer term with local associations, such as the Youth Club and Mothers' Association.

6.5   ENGAGEMENT AND IMPLEMENTATION

The Gorkha Earthquakes that hit Nepal in April and May 2015 prevented the Alliance from implementing these micro-projects in Lo Manthang. Furthermore, when in 2016 the Alliance tried to contact the Lopa students who participated in the November 2014 Workshop, all had moved to other parts of Nepal or emigrated outside Nepal. As a result, the Alliance decided to send a mission to Lo Manthang in 2016 with the DoA and Nepali and French experts to organize a public meeting with all representatives of the Lopa community in order to explain the benefits of documenting tangible cultural heritage. After the 2015 earthquakes, it was critical to commence documentation in order to allow access to funding from national authorities to implement easier and more accurate restoration or reconstruction works of damaged or destroyed public property. Furthermore, documentation would also provide a proof of ownership in case of illicit traffic, which has been frequently experienced by the Lopa community in the recent past.

The meeting was held in the public library at Lo Manthang and representatives from the local community were present, including monks from Choede Gompa, Amchi (Traditional Tibetan Doctor/healer) as well as the Youth Association, the ACAP and Women's Association. The DoA provided the Lopa community with a guarantee of accessibility to the documentation database and announced that it would hold a training session on inventory basics the following day through the organization of a hands-on inventorying exercise with Lopa participation on a public monument, which the Lopa community itself wished to select.

After learning the basic methodology of inventory exercise, the Lopa community decided to document a damaged chorten (*stupa*) inside the walled city. This was done by a group of Lopa people composed of youth, women and monks who worked on measuring the chorten and documenting the nature of damage. The DoA based its estimation for restoration on this documentation and decided to provide 50% of funds to the local community to start restoration. On the conclusion of the mission, stakeholders gave the impression that trust was established. In 2017 a major administrative and institutional change was implemented throughout Nepal and the former Village Development Committee (VDC) administering Upper Mustang from Jomsom was dissolved and replaced by a decentralized elected Municipal Council.

In winter of 2017–2018, the Lopa representatives who had restored the chorten went to Kathmandu to ask the DoA for the remaining 50% of the agreed amount. However, due to the new institutional structure, the fiscal year was over and the payment of this amount could not be made, thus generating a crisis which could jeopardize the confidence which the Alliance had tried to establish. A further mission was organized by the Alliance in May–June 2018 to monitor change in Lo Manthang with four experts from Nepal, China and France and four Nepali students from Khwopa Engineering College (Fig. 6.3). The Alliance invited the DoA to participate but the Lopa community refused to interact with the DoA unless payment of the remaining 50% spent for the chorten restoration was released as the local community had already

Fig. 6.3 Community engagement and reconstruction activities at Lo Manthang

advanced the funds and achieved the restoration in a manner that was deemed satisfactory by DoA experts.

Students and experts worked during one week to document changes outside and against the medieval earthen wall. They found that numerous new buildings were being erected around the walled city, proving a rapid and uncontrolled urban expansion. The following six basic parameters were identified for carrying out the physical survey of this expansion:

- Construction date;
- Number of stories; height
- Construction system (load bearing, reinforced cement concrete, mixed);
- Physical condition;
- Functional characteristics;
- Access to services (electricity, water supply and sanitation).

Out of the total 110 buildings surveyed, 63 are located on the eastern side, 18 on the southern, 23 on the western and 6 on the northern. Maps showing the materials drawn and the height and building use or function were elaborated. The total number of openings cut through the earthen sacred wall was also documented. Unstructured informal interviews were conducted with nine key Lopa people: one Vice-President of the Municipal Council, a monk, a school Principal and a Monastic School teacher, a farmer representing the Mothers' Group, a horseman, a carpenter, the owner of a guesthouse and the Representative of Mustang in Province 4 Parliament/Assembly in order to get an understanding of the local community's perceptions of heritage conservation and development of Lo Manthang.

6.6 Conclusion

In conclusion, working with the community is crucial as it reinforces local capacities, raises the awareness of the community, builds trust between stakeholders if, and only if, all legitimate interests are recognized and respected, and generates a shared long-term vision of heritage between stakeholders. It may require patience and effort but it is more fruitful and meaningful in the long run. While our focus in Lo Manthang is relatively new, our other projects in Nepal are gathering maturity and we are moving into phases of presentation. For example, a photobook entitled *Lumbini. Birthplace of Buddha*, was co-published with UNESCO (UNESCO 2013). Interpreting the uniqueness of the World Heritage property of Lumbini and its surroundings through 190 photographs taken by eight international photographers, it promotes the global importance of the special sacred and historic site of Lumbini.

Funding from the Alliance sponsored a second publication on Lumbini, *The Sacred Garden of Lumbini: Perceptions of Buddha's Birthplace* edited by Kai Weise (2013). Providing expert studies on eight realms of understanding of Lumbini: in Buddhist texts; in historical texts; in archaeology; as a planned site; as a World Heritage Property; in an environmental context; and in association with the activities and expectations of visitors, it helps define Lumbini's Outstanding Universal Value and presents recommended conservation and development guidelines for the management of the site. All these activities and experience demonstrate that even if governments are responsible for World Heritage inscription, they cannot be successful in managing and preserving their national cultural or natural heritage without the full support of local communities who are the best stewards of their own heritage once they are aware of its vulnerability and significance.

REFERENCES

Andolfatto, D. (2012). *An Inventory of the Buddhist Sites of the Kathmandu Valley (Nepal)*. Paris: Oriental Cultural Heritage Sites Protection Alliance.

Oriental Cultural Heritage Sites Protection Alliance, & Richon, M. (Eds.). (2018). *The Cultural Heritage of Nepal, Before, During and After the 2015 Earthquakes: Current and Future Challenges*. Kathmandu: Vajra Publications and Oriental Cultural Heritage Sites Protection Alliance.

Peissel, M. (1979). *Mustang: A Lost Tibetan Kingdom*. London: Futura Publications.

Selter, E. (2007). *Upper Mustang Cultural Heritage of Lo Tso Dhun*. Paris: UNESCO.

Slusser, M. S. (1982). *Nepal Mandala: A Cultural Study of the Kathmandu Valley*. Princeton: Princeton University Press.

Tucci, G. (1977). *Journey to Mustang 1952*. Kathmandu: Ratna Pustak Bhandar.

UNESCO. (2013). *Lumbini: Birthplace of Buddha*. Paris: UNESCO.

Weise, K. (Ed.). (2013). *The Sacred Garden of Lumbini: Perceptions of Buddha's Birthplace*. Kathmandu: UNESCO.

CHAPTER 7

Tourism and Community Engagement in World Heritage Sites, Nepal

Lisa Choegyal

Abstract Choegyal explores the complexities of managing sustainable tourism and community engagement at World Heritage Sites and in protected areas. Taking a destination management approach, she addresses the issues of tourism and community engagement from the perspective of stakeholders: resource managers, tourism industry, local residents and visitors. While acknowledging resource conservation must be paramount, Choegyal discusses the practicalities of planning for market-led sustainable tourism and product development. She examines suitable styles of tourism that can effectively involve communities and result in tangible benefits, employment and business opportunities for locals. Her experience concludes that partnerships often yield the best results. Choegyal ends with a case study of lessons learned at Lumbini in Nepal, the birthplace of Lord Buddha.

Keywords World Heritage Sites · Tourism · Lumbini

L. Choegyal (✉)
Kathmandu, Nepal
e-mail: lisa@choegyal.com

7.1   Introduction: Tourism as a Force for Conservation

Managing sustainable tourism and community engagement at World Heritage Sites (WHSs) and protected areas is complex. Tourism has often been seen by resource managers as a challenge instead of an opportunity to provide sites with coherent visitor management policies that can strengthen conservation and equitable local benefits. In recent years, development agencies, national and state tourist organisations, governments, and NGOs have realised that tourism can help achieve national objectives and deliver measurable results in employment creation, livelihood improvements and poverty reduction.

From my experience as an Asia-Pacific tourism specialist, it is clear that preservation and conservation of the physical, cultural and spiritual integrity of WHSs takes precedence over tourism. However, tourism can create a wide constituency of advocates whose interests are invested in the wellbeing of a site, and who can share collective custodial responsibility, ensuring its effective protection and appeal for visitors.

7.2   Tourism: Principles and Criteria

UNESCO's guiding principles are explicitly concerned with engaging local communities: to preserve, protect and present; respect sociocultural identity of host communities; and ensure sustainable, long-term development with benefits fairly distributed. Specifically, Article 5 of the 1972 UNESCO Convention calls on States Parties to 'adopt a general policy which aims to give the cultural and natural heritage a function in the life of the community' (https://whc.unesco.org/en/convention-text/). With social, religious, economic and environmental implications, communities must be integrally involved with sites and their management. Sustainable tourism can provide a rationale for protection of the site and, while it cannot solve every management issue, offer improvements to local livelihoods and visitor experiences.

UNESCO's objectives fit with ecotourism criteria and the UN's World Tourism Organization (UNWTO 2018) defines sustainable tourism as: 'Tourism that takes full account of its current and future economic, social and environmental impacts, addressing the needs of visitors, the industry, the environment and host communities' (http://sdt.unwto.org/content/about-us-5). While the terminology can be confusing (ecotourism, pro-poor, responsible, heritage/nature tourism, etc.), in developing countries the core message is that tourism interventions should protect nature and culture; benefit local people; and provide interpretation and education for visitors and host communities.

The key concept is that communities can participate in the process of deciding what tourism needs to achieve for their own aspirations, and in the best interest of their site, and how that affects the future. Too often WHSs react to visitor impacts, instead of proactively planning and shaping tourism to suit their needs.

Community tourism is best applied as an integral part of tourism destination planning and management processes. Although sites may have different sets of management issues, and specific solutions and outcomes, the principal of community engagement is universal. By taking a destination approach, the site has a better chance of success by gaining access to wider tourism industry networks, tourist patterns, visitor flows, and target source markets.

Acknowledging that local communities are central, many solutions can be gleaned from them, matching their ideas with market demand, current best practice and experience of what works and what doesn't elsewhere. Even if attuned to hospitality basics, local communities typically will have difficulty making links to markets and organising themselves to deliver quality services, and tourism experts can help.

Bringing together the many players around a table with a view to understanding each other's perspectives and agendas can have surprising and beneficial outcomes. Partnership approaches add value by together making development changes to protect a site that are more likely to succeed.

It is acknowledged that tourism, when properly managed, can be a force for conservation and create benefits for local people. Even though some may be intangible, indirect or hard to substantiate, when combined sustainable tourism presents a persuasive approach for site management:

- Tourism can create awareness and reinforce cultural and heritage values at a site in the eyes of local people and adjacent communities;
- Tourism can create direct economic values that provide clear rationales for nurturing and protecting the resource;
- Providing options for local people, tourism can diversify community jobs, supplement livelihoods, and revive dying and under-appreciated skills;

- Demand can be stimulated to generate new markets for local produce, food, arts and handicrafts;
- Tourism reinforces conservation values through education and interpretation, for both host communities and visiting guests;
- Tourism can improve and shape visitor behaviour at sites with guidelines of do's and don'ts;
- With tourism as the driver, infrastructure facilities, transportation and communications can be upgraded;
- Tourism helps to develop self-financing mechanisms for WHSs, providing the 'beating heart' that supplies lifeblood for site protection;
- Co-opting the tourism industry can widen advocacy for effective site management, motivated by the protection of a resource on which their business depends.

7.3   TAKING A DESTINATION APPROACH

WHS managers may not be experts in tourism or community engagement but they need to know the language and understand the principles of both. Taking a destination approach involves the inclusion of the wider tourism industry, setting the attractions of WHSs into an overall tourism context, thereby co-opting a broader base of supporters invested in its success. This wide circle of players is likely to include:

- Core decision makers, resource and protected area managers, appropriate departments, and officials from national and regional governments;
- National and local tourism organisations, and industry associations;
- Non-Governmental Organisations concerned with conservation, tourism or community development;
- Transportation operators;
- International, national and local tour operators and ground handlers;
- Infrastructure managers in nearby towns and cities;
- Neighbouring attraction operators;
- Accommodation providers;
- Food and drink providers and retailers;
- Shops and souvenir outlets;
- Local producers, farmers and handicraft makers;
- Tour guides;

- Academics;
- Funders;
- Visitors.

To be effective in destination management, it is necessary to understand visitors, as well as the products and attractions. This includes:

- Who they are, where they come from, where they stay, what they are looking for, how they travel, etc.;
- Analysing market segments, recognising that different visitors have a variety of motivations;
- Developing products to match markets, ensuring that attractions meet visitor needs and deliver overall WHS destination images;
- Planning proactively, using market research and community representation from the outset;
- Linking with mainstream tourism circuits, acknowledging that WHSs are part of a wider network;
- Forging partnerships, ensuring a crossover of agendas from as wide a range of stakeholders as possible, including resource managers, tourism industry and local community;
- Recognise that visitor safety and security are a prerequisite for successful tourism.

7.4   ENGAGING WITH COMMUNITIES

Community engagement must understand the related communities and see resources through their eyes. Analysis can be described in a matrix of various stakeholders and their agendas. Community engagement specialists use techniques and social mobilisation tools that include participatory rural appraisals, rapid rural appraisals, appreciative participatory planning and action, and resource mapping. Consultations can lead to a range of solutions with the objective of empowering communities in order to encourage their participation in aspects of resource management, protection and tourism.

The purpose of these exercises is to understand community stakeholders; analyse community perspectives and agendas, and see how they can meaningfully relate to sustainable tourism activities; coordinate with social mobilisation and resource mapping specialists to incorporate their recommendations; and undertake consultations and trainings with the objective of empowering and capacitating community participation in sustainable tourism.

Lessons were learned from Nepal's Tourism for Rural Poverty Alleviation Programme (TRPAP), an investment of almost $5 million between 2001 and 2006, in which community participation in tourism was central (Dhakal et al. 2007). TRPAP trialled and developed product models and institutional mechanisms appropriate for sustainable rural tourism at village, district and national levels. To contribute to poverty alleviation, participatory techniques were used to involve government officials and local bodies in rural tourism development, to strengthen environmental conservation, empower disadvantaged groups and women, and for social mobilisation. Participatory approaches involving all stakeholders from the early planning stages ensured that community tourism initiatives were more effective and sustainable than those imposed by outsiders. Reported as a 'well thought out, ambitious pro-poor tourism programme', certain aspects were reviewed as 'Mildly Unsatisfactory', including 'how far tourism related micro-enterprise development work had been effective in the rural areas' and 'whether tourism market linkages initiated by the programme had been effective', with one area, 'how far tourism related micro-enterprise development work had been effective in the rural areas', graded 'Unsatisfactory' (Bhattarai et al. 2006: iv).

7.5   PRACTICAL AND PRAGMATIC APPROACHES

Practical and business-like money-making techniques are needed for successful community tourism. With financial viability as a prerequisite, people protect the resource on which the business depends and collaborate closely with neighbours in areas such as employment, guiding and local produce.

Markets are increasingly sensitive to ensuring that their tourism dollar goes to good use, especially in poor and developing nations. When sympathetically targeted with respectfully pitched expectations, tourism can effectively provide supplementary income for villagers, both directly and indirectly, and opportunities for small businesses. In addition, market demand is met by providing unique, 'authentic' and 'real' interpersonal interpreted experiences demanded by higher-paying and longer-stay visitors, 'bringing alive' a destination, and cementing a satisfying 'host and guest' balance.

Ideas for tourism interventions that engage and benefit communities in Asian destinations include:

- Introducing tourism of a scale and style that can involve local people;
- Adapting traditional practices for tourists such as vernacular architecture and local furniture and materials to create unique ambiances;
- Promoting local produce in accommodation and restaurants in response to most markets seeking something special, with a consciousness of food miles and wellness concerns;
- Developing everyday activities into tourism products such as local transportation, homestays and cooking, guided village house and temple visits, religious festivals and sports events, and participation in agricultural activities recognising that visitors increasingly seek authentic and active experiences;
- Matching products with markets;
- Developing high-quality interpretation and guiding using on-site trained local guides, that can ensure that the community 'takes control of the story', telling traditional myths and legends, and showcasing with pride their culture and heritage;
- Supplementing a community's lack of tourism or marketing skills with a collaboration of partners in order to identify potential products and services, and to reach markets.

7.6 Partnerships to Manage Impacts

Academic papers have noted positive and negative impacts of tourism on communities. A range of sophisticated rating systems and criteria are being developed, including UNESCO's own visitor management assessment tool which attempts to quantify sustainability as a percentage scoring system against governance/management, economic, social/cultural and environmental impacts, and tourism's contribution to site protection as measured against UN's Sustainable Development Goals (Debrine 2018; UNESCO World Heritage and Sustainable Tourism Programme 2018). Examples of economic, social and environmental impacts on Asian communities have included:

- Litter, waste and air/water pollution from poor management practices;
- Structural/physical damage to WHSs from crowding or unmanaged visitor patterns;
- Compromising the sanctity or cultural value of a site by uncontrolled development or conflicting visitor use;
- Wildlife disturbance and habituation of species, resulting in harmful changes to wildlife behaviour or competition for resources;
- User conflicts over water, power and land use;
- Rising land and commodity prices caused by tourism demand;
- Unrealistic expectations leading to disappointment and disenchantment in tourism by host communities;
- Visitor fatigue and disillusionment due to crowding/overuse.

'Overtourism' has received increasing attention as communities complain of being overwhelmed by visitor numbers, resulting in pressure on resources and infrastructure (Milano et al. 2018). The solution to these undesirable impacts may be found in effective planning and partnerships for management and marketing that disperses tourism flows, manages seasonality, pitches expectations, or controls visitation with techniques such as tiered pricing, restricted timing, or controlled transportation and access. What ultimately counts is that communities receive benefits from the conservation of the resource, and a harmonious and sustainable partnership exists between resource managers, stakeholder communities and the tourism industry.

7.7   Case Study: Tourism at Lumbini World Heritage Site, Nepal

There are lessons to be learned about the pitfalls of tourism and local community interaction from Lumbini, the birthplace of Gautama Buddha, listed in 1997 as a UNESCO WHS and located in Nepal's lowland Terai, 26 kilometres or half an hour drive west of Bhairahawa.

Archaeologist Anton Führer and the Governor of Palpa in West Nepal, Khadga Shamsher, rediscovered Lumbini's Asokan Pillar in 1896 (Weise 2013). Lumbini's archaeological sites, the Mayadevi Temple that enshrines the marker stone and the museum are maintained and managed by the Lumbini Development Trust (LDT) (ICOMOS

Nepal 2013) (Fig. 7.1). Surrounded by Muslim and Hindu villages, Lumbini is an integral part of the Footsteps of the Lord Buddha spiritual pilgrimage sites directly associated with the Buddha's life in Bihar and Uttar Pradesh, India.

A total of 1.55 million visitors visited the WHS in 2017, growth of 17% over 2016, of which the bulk were 1.25 million Nepali domestic visitors. Indian visitors increased 14% to 155,444, and third country international visitors grew 7% to 145,796 visitors (LDT 2018). Despite healthy growth, Greater Lumbini Area (GLA) visitor patterns feature short stays, mostly less than one-day visits, and low expenditure. Visitors, especially non-pilgrims, report not enough to do, poor maintenance and a paucity of information (Ministry of Finance and DFID 2018). Effective linkages with local communities are yet to be achieved, although there is potential for handicrafts and some hotels offer guided village visits by bicycle.

Fig. 7.1   Mahadevi Temple at Lumbini, birthplace of Lord Buddha

Lumbini suffers from seasonal constraints due to hot, humid and wet summers from April to October. Air pollution from neighbouring industrial plants and Indian brick factories is not only unhealthy and unsightly, but undermines the peaceful sanctity of the site and threatens its spiritual value (IUCN 2012) (Fig. 7.2). The challenge is not only to extend visitor stay with improved facilities and attractions that strengthen its spirituality, but also to ensure that Muslim and Hindu communities around Lumbini reap benefits from tourism.

Lumbini featured as a TRPAP site between 2001 and 2006, seeking to mainstream community engagement in tourism. Village tours were introduced to disperse visitor patterns with demonstrations of handicraft making (clay sculptures and Tharu basketry) and showcase local culture in Rupandehi District. This was widely advertised on tourist information boards at Lumbini, in travel brochures and on websites. Tourists were encouraged to hire rickshaws and bicycles from the local people and

Fig. 7.2 Industrial plant near Lumbini

thus, through TRPAP, some villages started receiving limited benefits from tourists for the first time (Dhakal et al. 2007).

The Greater Lumbini Area 2015–2024 Tourism Promotion Plan (GLTPP MoCTCA 2015) study reports that international visitors stay an average of 1.8 days, 90% overnighters, spending an average of $67 per visit (day visitors spend an average of $8). In contrast, Indians average only 0.09 days, just a couple of hours, with 90% being day visitors spending an average of $4 per visit (overnighters spend $46). Domestic visitors stay 0.7 days, average spend by overnighters $31 and $6 per day visit. The Ministry of Culture, Tourism and Civil Aviation (MoCTCA) reported that Sunauli near Bhairahawa is Nepal's most popular land border accounting for 84% of all land arrivals to Nepal in 2017 and used by 150,841 international visitors (MoCTCA 2018). This figure includes arrivals to Lumbini, although it is reported that many same day international visitors to Lumbini avoid paying the Nepal entry visa and are not recorded. Public transport arrangements from the border to Lumbini are rudimentary and most visitors arrive on packages with Indian transport operators.

The Greater Lumbini nine site circuit includes Tilaurakot, identified by many as ancient Kapilvastu, and containing the conserved remains of palaces and shrines together with a small museum. Other sites are Kudan, Gotihawa, Niglihawa, Sagarhawa, Aurorakot, Devadaha and Ramagrama, the latter believed to be the repository of one-eighth of the Lord Buddha's cremated remains. There is little reliable arrival data for these sites but informal estimates report several hundred visitors daily during the clement winter months, and many local visitors. The circuit has been developed in response to the need to extend visitor stay in the GLA but most sites still lack appeal for non-Buddhists.

7.8   Lumbini: Increasing Tourism Potential

As discussed at a recent UNESCO and KOICA sponsored workshop in Kathmandu in 2018, the imperative at Lumbini is to extend the season and attract a broader spectrum of pilgrim and non-pilgrim visitors (UNESCO and KOICA 2018). To achieve this, a wider range of accommodation facilities are needed, as are more attractions, improved interpretation and better transport. The multinational monasteries in Lumbini could play a more active role in tourism, contributing teachings, meditation sessions and other activities for pilgrims and cultural tourists.

Although the response from some surrounding villages indicates a lack of aptitude for direct tourism engagement, community representatives do interact with LDT and the tourism industry, and there is potential for local produce, handicrafts and village visits.

Marketing and promotion is urgently needed for the GLA not only to spread tourism benefits to local communities but also to create further awareness and a desire to visit for new markets, to lengthen the stay and increase the spend of current visitors, and to address seasonality issues.

The following current and potential target segments have been identified for the WHS and GLA destinations. Due to lack of data, it is not possible to accurately quantify either arrivals or expenditure, but assumptions have been made based on general Nepal tourism statistics and industry feedback.

7.8.1   Nepal Domestic—Leisure and Pilgrimage

Nepalis on short breaks with increasing disposable income and time offer a proven demand for pilgrimage visits, picnics and leisure breaks as 1.25 million visited Lumbini in 2017, a significant growth of 19% from 2016. Constrained by lack of facilities, improved products will appeal to new domestic segments, with future potential for non-resident Nepalis, and visiting friends and relatives. Future domestic targets include more pilgrimage, business, family and friends, and couples and retreat groups. Domestic visitors are a key segment heavily relied on by many tourism businesses.

7.8.2   Indian—Pilgrimage, Cross Border and Self-Drive

New international air linkages to India and an estimated 35 million urban middle-class Indians living in 11 major cities within eight hours drive of Nepal's border with a tradition of hill station breaks, also offer potential. Currently, border towns rely on Indian business operators and Indian pilgrims visit Nepal's Hindu temples including Muktinath and Pashupatinath. However, Indians to Lumbini currently have the shortest stay and lowest expenditure, attracting only 155,000 Indians in 2017 (LDT 2018). Improved products and facilities will attract new and higher spending Indian segments, such as the new 102-room five-star Tiger Palace Resort and Casino near Bhairahawa, which is successfully targeting Indian families and groups as well as weddings and honeymooners.

7.8.3   *International Pilgrims*

The birthplace of Lord Buddha is one of the most important Buddhist pilgrimage destinations. Lumbini received 146,000 international (non-Indian) visitors in 2017, a small percentage of the world's 535 million Buddhists. The GLA's nine sites have potential to attract a wider range of nationalities and new segments with the upcoming ADB funded international airport at Bhairahawa providing potential air links to the Indian pilgrimage sites of Bodhgaya, Varanasi and Kushinagar (ADB 2006; IFC and Government of India 2013; IFC and Investment Board Nepal 2013), and improved attractions, such as a rebuilt Mayadevi Temple, a more suitably spiritual atmosphere, the completed visitor centre, a revitalised museum, and international brand accommodation. Likewise, visitation to the wide range of important Hindu pilgrimage sites within reach of Lumbini would be stimulated by increased awareness and improved facilities.

7.8.4   *International Pre-booked General Interest*

Usually travelling with Kathmandu travel agencies, pre-booked via international tour operator networks or directly on websites, these 'high-end explorers' from Western and Asian countries seek authentic cultural experiences and care about community benefits and environmental conservation. Currently, this sector has low interest in Lumbini, citing not enough to see and do. Improved community products, services and interpretation are needed, and circuit patterns to include the GLA, beyond the current Kathmandu, Pokhara, Chitwan triangle in combination with Syangja, Tansen Palpa along the Siddhartha Highway will help.

7.8.5   *International Special Interest*

Groups and individuals motivated by special interest activities include Buddhist study groups, wildlife and bird watching, community activities and cultural experiences such as festivals, visits to Lumbini sites and temples, art and museums groups, artisans and handicrafts, study tours, and sporting events, such as the recently promoted Lumbini Peace Marathon. Although currently a small segment, there is potential with improved guiding, information and facilities.

7.8.6   *International Foreign Independent Travellers (FITs)—Backpackers, Budget Explorers*

About half of Nepal's third country (non-Indian) foreign visitors travel individually, comprising Western and Asian nationalities. Although most are budget travellers and trekkers, FITs use public transport and community homestays, have long stay patterns and a proven interest in new destinations and village products. Many overland travellers from India use the Sunauli border crossing, although currently Lumbini attracts few FITs due to lack of appeal or transport.

7.9   CONCLUSION

Tourism solutions can bring vitality to the GLA as a successful sacred attraction, including partnerships to achieve a cohesive marketing strategy, well organised community-based attractions and careful destination management. Recent archaeological finds have brought world attention to the birthplace of Lord Buddha and there are opportunities for local guides, story-telling and interpretation to bring alive the spirituality of the WHS for both religious and more general-interest visitors. Improved product ideas include an upgraded museum and visitor centre, a daily ceremony opening and closing the Mayadevi Temple, walking and biking trail along Queen Maya's Path linking Tilaurakot with Lumbini, an evening sound and light show depicting the life of Prince Siddhartha, and an architectural competition to replace the temporary Mayadevi Temple structure. This will best be achieved in stakeholder partnerships that involve government, private sector and adjacent communities.

REFERENCES

ADB. (2006). *Preparing the South Asia Subregional Economic Cooperation Tourism Development Project: Technical Assistance Report*. https://www.adb.org/sites/default/files/project-document/66589/39399-reg-tar.pdf.

Bhattarai, S., Adhikari, S. R., & Bamford, D. (2006). *Tourism for Rural Poverty Alleviation Programme (TRPAP) (NEP/99/013): Final Evaluation Report*. Unpublished Report.

Debrine, P. (2018). *UNESCO World Heritage and Sustainable Tourism*. Presentation at Planning and Orientation Workshop World Heritage Journeys to Buddhist Sites in Kathmandu, Nepal.

Dhakal, D. P., Khadka, M., Sharma, S., & Choegyal, L. (2007). *Lessons Learned: Nepal's Experience Implementing Sustainable Rural Tourism Development Model: Submitted to Tourism for Rural Poverty Alleviation Programme (TRPAP)*. http://www.np.undp.org/content/nepal/en/home/library/poverty/lessons-learned–nepal-s-experience-implementing-sustainable-rur.html.

ICOMOS (Nepal). (2013). *Heritage Impact Assessment of Tourism on Lumbini World Heritage Property*. http://unesdoc.unesco.org/images/0022/002264/226404e.pdf.

IFC and Government of India. (2013). *Investing in the Buddhist Circuit 2014–2018*. https://www.ifc.org/wps/wcm/connect/a0b004004618b490804eb99916182e35/Buddhist+Circuit+Tourism+Strategy+Final.pdf?MOD=AJPERES.

IFC and Investment Board Nepal. (2013). *Identifying Investment Opportunities for Cultural Tourism in Nepal Final Report Including Projects in Tansen Palpa and Greater Lumbini*. Unpublished Report.

IUCN (Nepal). (2012). *Environmental Impact Assessment of Industrial Development Around Lumbini, the Birthplace of Lord Buddha*. World Heritage Property, Kathmandu. http://unesdoc.unesco.org/images/0021/002196/219616e.pdf.

Lumbini Development Trust. (2018). *Tourism Statistics 2017*. Kathmandu: LDT.

Milano, C., Cheer, J. M., & Novelli, M. (2018). *Overtourism: A Growing Global Problem*. http://theconversation.com/overtourism-a-growing-global-problem-100029.

Ministry of Finance and DFID. (2018). *Scoping Study on Tourism Opportunities in Pokhara to Sunauli Economic Corridor Nepal*. Unpublished Report.

MoCTCA. (2015). *Greater Lumbini Tourism Promotion Plan (GLTPP) (2015–2024), LDT/ADB/SATIDP, Loan and Grant No L2579; G0179*. Unpublished Report.

MoCTCA. (2018). *Nepal Tourism Statistics 2017*. http://tourism.gov.np/files/statistics/2.pdf.

UNESCO. (1972). *Convention Concerning the Protection of the World Cultural and Natural Heritage*. https://whc.unesco.org/en/conventiontext/.

UNESCO and KOICA. (2018). *Situation Analysis and Tourism Needs Assessment for the Buddhist Heritage Route for Sustainable Tourism Development in South Asia at Paharpur, Sanchi, and Greater Lumbini*. Unpublished Report.

UNESCO World Heritage and Sustainable Tourism Programme. (2018). http://whc.unesco.org/en/tourismtoolkit.

UNWTO. (2018). http://sdt.unwto.org/content/about-us-5.

Weise, K. (Ed.). (2013). *The Sacred Garden of Lumbini: Perceptions of Buddha's Birthplace*. Kathmandu: UNESCO.

CHAPTER 8

Mapping the Intangible: 'At Risk' Heritage Landscapes in Northern Pakistan

Zahra Hussain

Abstract Hussain introduces the centrality of local communities in the preservation of intangible heritage by focusing on the community, culture and heritage nexus. Approaching intangible heritage as the cultural practices and living patterns of communities, this chapter explores the importance of preserving heritage landscapes in the aftermath of crisis, conflicts and disasters. It introduces a participatory mapping project in post-disaster areas in northern Pakistan and illustrates how local communities can be involved in the process of documenting and preserving their own intangible heritage landscapes.

Keywords Pakistan · Community · Heritage · Language patterns

8.1 Introduction

Conflicts and disasters place South Asia heritage at risk (Jigyasu 2016; Biagioli and Maria-Olivieri 2014). They also pose threats to intangible cultural heritage with Oliver-Smith explaining that often disaster

Z. Hussain (✉)
Laajverd, Islamabad, Pakistan

© The Author(s) 2019
R. Coningham and N. Lewer (eds.), *Archaeology, Cultural Heritage Protection and Community Engagement in South Asia*,
https://doi.org/10.1007/978-981-13-6237-8_8

resettlement interventions "endanger the connection that people have with their built environment, violating cultural norms of space and place, inhibiting the re-weaving of social networks and delaying or stopping the re-emergence of community identity" (2006: 23). Cultural practices emerge from interactions between nature, culture, beliefs and world-views embedded in the cultural landscape (Taylor and Lennon 2011), while spatial patterns are configurations devised in built environments with regard to climate, culture and belief systems developed over generations (Salingaros 2006). They are part of intangible heritage, requiring deep engagement and analysis that is not always visible and cannot be easily captured. These practices and patterns are usually ignored in post-disaster resettlement scenarios, creating new forms of uncertainty and displacement.

This chapter will discuss a mapping project in post-disaster areas in northern Pakistan, which seeks to document cultural practices of everyday life and the built environment. Elaborating on the project's participatory nature, it highlights the methods used by participants in the Laajverd Visiting School (LVS) to engage communities in documenting practices and spatial patterns in villages in the Gojal Valley in Gilgit-Baltistan (Fig. 8.1). It illustrates how local communities can be involved in the process of generating, producing, reflecting and exchanging knowledge.

Fig. 8.1 Map of the Gojal Valley

8.2   HERITAGE—COMMUNITY NEXUS

Encapsulated by UNESCO's 2003 *Convention for the Safeguarding of the Intangible Cultural Heritage*, Kurin explains that living heritage is "practiced and expressed by members of cultural communities through such forms as oral traditions, song, performance, rituals, craftsmanship and artistry and systems of knowledge" (2007: 12). As such, intangible heritage can be located in the cultural landscape of communities, where both are understood as heterogeneous and dynamic entities. People develop relations with their social and natural environments through practices, knowledges and skills passed on from one generation to the next, culminating in an intangible heritage repository (Blake 2009). Intangible heritage is expressed through practices, oral traditions, rituals and modes of being and living of people in a particular landscape (Kurin 2007; Munjeri 2009). To explore this, we can engage with the notion of cultural landscapes that encompasses relations between people and their land and environment giving rise to unique modes of existence.

8.3   CULTURAL LANDSCAPES

Cultural landscapes are constituted by inhabitants as they engage with the landscape to "make it relevant for their own lives, strategies and project" (Rose 2002: 457). While tangible aspects can be assessed through material culture, objects, sites and built environment, the intangible is associated with the cultural practices and living patterns of a community. As cultural landscapes emerge through the entanglement of social, culture, economic and natural processes and practices, they also undergo change due to reasons including economic and social shifts associated with globalization, new technologies, conflicts and disasters.

These changes involve reinterpretation of norms and values related with particular practices or expectations associated with gender roles but this reinterpretation is not sudden or in isolation. Reinterpretation involves constant negotiation, resistance, and contestations over a time, where access to knowledge, power and mobility play important roles. It is therefore important to establish that while cultural landscapes are not static entities, neither are their communities homogenous. Therefore, communities must be understood as "social creations and experiences that continuously in motion, rather than fixed entities and descriptions" (Waterton and Smith 2010: 8–9).

To conduct an exercise in mapping intangible heritage within a cultural landscape, it is important to understand what it entails. Different kinds of practice play a part in forming intangible cultural heritage that can be addressed through Ingold's 'dwelling perspective', where "the landscape is constituted as an enduring record of, and testimony to, the lives and works of past generations who have dwelt within it" (1993: 152). How people carry out everyday life in a landscape can help us examine the relations between the natural, social and cultural entities that form landscapes over time (ibid.: 195). Everyday practices and movement in and around home and land are informed by geographic landscapes, seasonal routines and climatic conditions, exemplifying deep correspondence. This develops over time as practices and processes are attuned to environments, and environments are morphed and created in response. How people belong in this emergent landscape is by re-inscribing their practices of everyday life, by establishing continual relations to the surroundings weaving an intricate web of relations between places, practices, memories and identities that not only performed but also embodied (Bennett 2012).

While there are temporal and spatial dimensions to experiencing modes of belonging, active belonging-in-place occurs through relational practices which occur as people begin to associate with, or abstain from something. In this sense, belonging is not experienced in spatial or temporal confinements, rather established through relations of different practices. For example, women in Kashmir's Neelum Valley described how they feel a certain attachment and belonging to their house through practices such as "applying layer of mud plaster every morning after dawn, hence maintaining and caring for it" (Field notes LVS 2015).

The skills, knowledge, decisions and relations through which built forms emerge, and are maintained, form an intrinsic part of a cultural landscape's intangible heritage. Built forms bear traces of the past but also exemplify relations between environment, climate, geography, culture, religion, tasks, and skills that generate a specific form. Ingold explains that "the forms people build....arise within the current of their involved activity, the specific relational contexts of their practical engagement with their surrounding" (2000: 186). In this sense, house construction entails similar correspondence informing the spatial form of the dwelling unit, its surroundings and the entire settlement and plays an important role in who we are and how everyday life is lived (Stevens 2012: 588). In spatial theory, this can be approached through the concept of 'Pattern Language', which contains rules for how human beings interact with built forms and codifies practical solutions developed over millennia (Alexander et al. 1977). Alexander lays great stress on 'reciprocity' between different *forces* due to which patterns are formed highlighting how inhabitants' partake of the construction of environment-valuing tradition and a shared design language (1979). Spatial arrangements are not only informed by people's movements but also seasonal conditions, terrain and the sun, wind and soil. It is a unique correspondence system developed in conjunction of available materials, skill-sets, social practices, religious beliefs and seasonal conditions that lead to a distinct mode of gathering that become part of a landscape's intangible heritage. As opposed to the often rigid and uniform production of architectural space due to modernization, patterns emerge as a result of how space is organically arranged and developed in a context through the interrelations of culture, religion, climate and landscape, unique to different regions and cultures.

Pattern languages thus form part of intangible heritage, not as a product of built form but a 'living' process (Seitel 2001: 13). It also relates to how spaces might be organized and used by men and women differently. For example, in a traditional one-room Pamiri house, women occupy the centrally located stove area throughout the day for making tea, food and entertaining guests. When this central position was compromised by disaster resettlement houses with separate kitchens, women felt alienated (Field notes LVS 2017). Community senses of belonging, place-making and personal and social capacities are linked to these everyday practices and spatial patterns. Therefore, before any intervention or development, these practices and patterns must be considered. In order to map or document them, it is crucial to employ participatory methodologies where communities can narrate their living processes, priorities, challenges and requirements given the emerging context.

8.4 The Laajverd Visiting School and Creative-Participatory Action Research

The 'Indigenous Practices and Patterns Catalog' (IPPC) is a mapping programme initiated by the LVS during an annual two-week action research exercise in prone/post-disaster and post-conflict landscapes with mountain communities of northern Pakistan. Since 2014, mapping has been conducted in Gilgit-Baltistan, Azad Kashmir and Khyber

Pakhtunkhwa Provinces. The LVS employs creative and participatory methodologies of working with local communities and engaging with the understanding that ideas of "a homogenous community" is under scrutiny (Cole 2005; Watson 2007; Waterton and Smith 2009). Another underlying critique of assessing intangible heritage is identified in the divide between heritage experts and local communities, where the expert carries out representation (Waterton and Smith 2010). The LVS engages with the knowledge, skills and practices of 'source community' (Peers and Brown 2007: 519), where intangible heritage is based on and performed through the practices of everyday life and through the relations between living spaces and the environment exemplifying the interrelations, interdependencies and adaptation between nature and the peoples. Local communities are thus integral to mapping and are engaged throughout the process, from identification, documentation to the compilation of the data.

LVS' mapping exercise is designed under the 'Creative-Participatory Action Research' (C-PAR) introduced during 2015, a combination of different methodologies such as empirical walks, photography with local people, tea sessions, documentation and drawings, conversations, spending time with craftspersons, and listening to stories narrated by elders or simply doing things with locals. This participatory exercise involves conducting research with locals, rather than on them, in order to explore and encompass their knowledge, experience, priorities and concerns (Kindon 2010). As mentioned, local communities are the prime narrators of their landscapes and to understand these in depth, formal interviews and informal conversations are used to help investigate social fabric and cultural capital. Mapping also includes diagramming exercises with communities as a method that allows 'marginal groups to voice their previously muted "standpoint" in ways that can disrupt the smooth reproduction of dominant discourses and practices' (Kesby 2000: 425).

The 'creative' aspect of our methodology is aimed at encouraging LVS participants to experiment with different data collection methods and employ these interchangeably. Documenting cultural practices is always a challenge since these are an intrinsic part of everyday lives and identities, hence each and every act cannot be known and narrated. Therefore, LVS participants are encouraged to employ methods for accessing the cultural landscape. For example, female LVS researchers may join a cooking session with a local woman to converse about historic festivities as well as observe the practice of cooking. In this sense, methods respond to contextual conditions rather than the will of the researcher, allowing mapping to be participatory and sensitive to context. While mapping the cultural practices and spatial patterns of mountain communities in northern Pakistan, a combination of the following methods was used.

Walking Talks: Mapping usually begins with walking around neighbourhoods and having impromptu conversations with people to begin engaging with them. This allows researchers to become acquainted with the area and establish relationships with locals. The walk continues as more locals join and help provoke site-specific responses allowing researchers to observe surroundings, and for the locals to revisit and recollect their knowledge about certain techniques of construction or materials. This information ranges from place-based orientations to practices of landscape. For example, why a certain place is a landmark, sacred or important in the community or, how the community collectively builds water channels and pathways every year. While walking in Gulmit village in the Gojal Valley, our walk included concentration points, such as a 200-year-old house now used as a carpet-weaving centre. Here, locals explained the process of constructing traditional houses with local materials, while highlighting the spiritual significance and practical benefits of low-height doors and open-plan traditional houses.

Tea Sessions: Another method of engagement, particularly with community women, occurs through tea sessions. Within the rich hospitality culture of Pakistan's northern Valleys, guests are invited to tea and these become modes of engaging with local knowledge (Thompson 2008; Kovach 2009). They are often accompanied by storytelling, where elders respond to queries and narrate stories of places, rituals and historical way of doing and being in the landscape. These instances are crucial for mapping as the community themselves narrate their intangible heritage (Fig. 8.2).

Community Mapping: Mapping allows participants to visually represent the ideas, information and emotions they hold with regard to space (Downs and Stea 1974; Kitchin 1994). Community mapping is a form of mental mapping (Kitchin 1994) and a method to investigate locals' ideas, 'sense of place' and notions of dwelling, interpretation and moving in the landscape. The maps convey a weave of interrelations and lived experience of landscape through qualitative, artistic and creative modes of representation ranging from drawings, maps, embroideries, and mosaics (Grasseni 2012: 100). They illustrate daily and seasonal practices of local communities, highlighting festivals, rituals and everyday tasks. For

Fig. 8.2   LVS tea session with women

example, the map below shows the daily and seasonal routines of women in Sarat village, highlighting prioritized tasks and festivals associated with seasonal activities (Fig. 8.3).

Discursive Sessions: This is a crucial phase of the documentation process, when the data is compiled and examined with local communities, as they create platforms for engagement and exchange that allow locals to

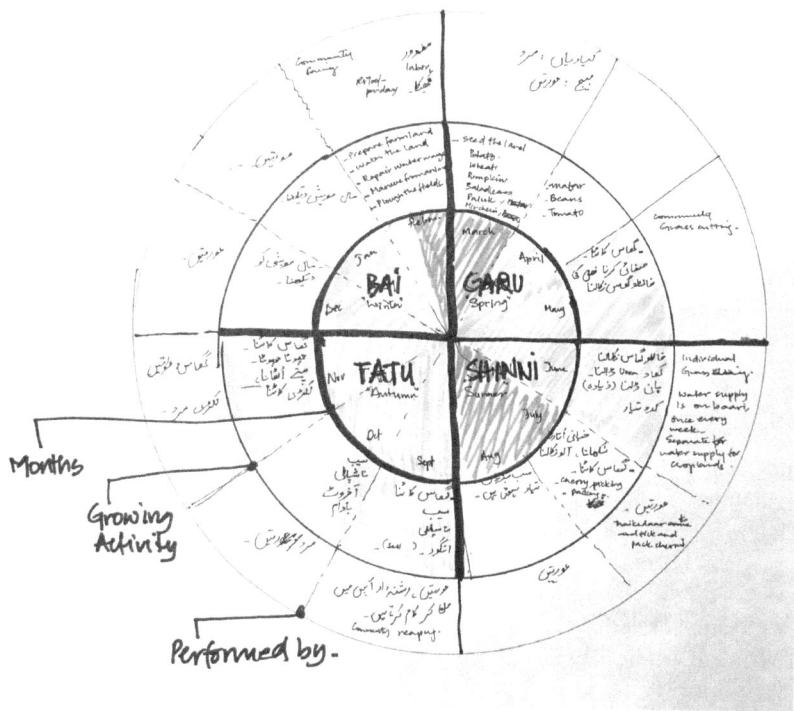

Fig. 8.3 Community map of daily and seasonal routines of women at Sarat

see the compilation of their practices and architectural patterns but also add to them. Here, lost and dying intangible heritage are also identified and added to the repository. This becomes a reflective session for local community to revisit their everyday practices through the repository and assess the threats and challenges to their intangible heritage. During discussions, they also highlight how intangible heritage is transforming and the impacts it has on their socio-cultural and natural environments. In this sense, not only is the local community involved in mapping but also in narrating the changing context of intangible heritage in their cultural landscapes. These practices and patterns range from a dwelling unit to the entire landscape, highlighting daily and seasonal practices of communities. This information is collated in the form of the IPPC, which is a collection of text, drawings and photographs.

8.5   *DISPATCHES* FROM THE FIELD

Our 2017 LVS focused on the Gojal Valley under the theme 'Mapping Resilience' to understand how local communities maintain their cultural landscapes in the midst of increased challenges, including natural hazards and disasters. Alongside these threats and the potential relocation of communities, the development of mega-infrastructure projects, such as the China-Pakistan Economic Corridor (CPEC), is also playing a significant role in the transformation of cultural landscapes due to new roads and increased tourism. During our mapping, the local community noted the transformation of the built environment of their village, particularly along the main CPEC-funded road in the form of small hotels and guesthouses designed in contrast to traditional housing.

The resettlement of displaced persons from the Attabad Landslide Disaster in Shishket Village also challenges traditional pattern language and their meanings. During a tea session, women discussed issues and challenges faced after the disaster, which displaced 400 households. They expressed how food consumption patterns have been transformed as World Food Programme packs with higher daily sugar intakes have increased body weights. Locals also shared how the lack of vegetables and grain has led people to buy bakery items, resulting in detrimental health. One man observed family consumption changes from communal consumption of a daily *phitti* (thick circular bread) to individual bread slices (Field notes LVS 2014). When the conversation moved to living patterns, the inadequate design of resettlement house was highlighted in comparison with the pattern of traditional houses based on open-plan with central hearth and skylight/ventilator with the roof supported by five columns, known as *Panjetan*. The concept of *Punjetan* denotes a strong spiritual significance for the Shia-Ismaili community in Gilgit-Baltistan (Cheema 2007). The hearth or fireplace is usually located in the centre to equally distribute heat accompanied by raised platforms of varying heights used for sitting, sleeping, guests and musicians (Field notes LVS 2014). The open-plan spatial typology reflects the rich culture of hospitality that forms an intrinsic part of their identity and being able to host guests in the everyday, and conduct festivity in the house. Resettlement houses were described by locals as a 'box with divisions' (Field notes LVS 2017), compromising traditional spatial patterns and cultural practices.

The IPPC can also serve as a cultural heritage repository to be accessed by researchers, developers and local community during interventions and development initiatives. For example, the 2017 LVS IPPC was crucial in designing a community heritage museum in the Laspur Valley. LVS' architects iterated traditional architectural pattern language according to the contextual requirements and designed the museum as an octagon around five columns; the sides of octagon serve as themed walls and the five columns denote the *Punjetan* (Fig. 8.4). The tradition of central skylight was maintained but the roof, which is traditionally flat, has been redesigned at a forty-five-degree slant as requested by local community for clearing snow. Hence, the museum's artefacts narrate the cultural histories of Laspur and its design offers an expression of the cultural heritage which the community presents to visitors. When contemporary requirements were met with slight iterations, the community still

Fig. 8.4 **a** Heritage Museum at Laspur. **b** Sketch of Heritage Museum at Laspur showing how the five columns pattern is used in the traditional form of house construction

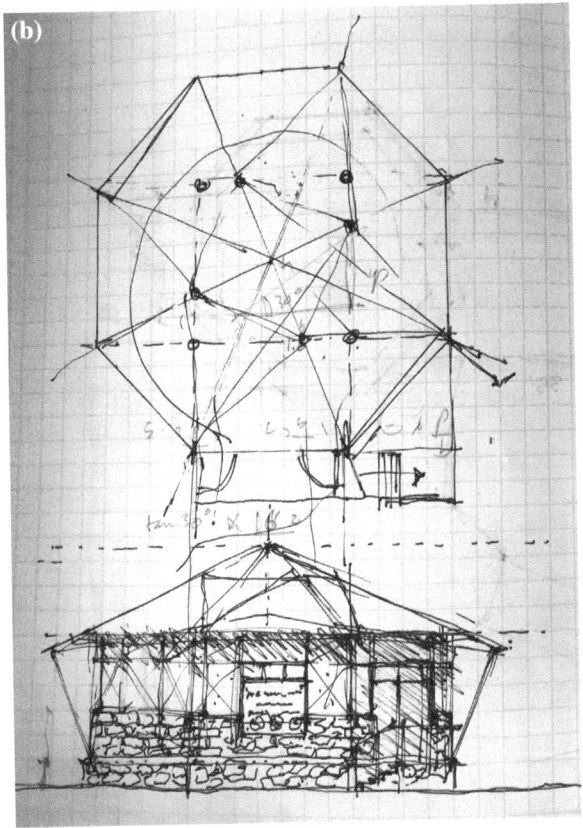

Fig. 8.4 (continued)

felt a sense of pride in how their cultural heritage can accompany the changing present.

8.6   CONCLUSION

Tangible and intangible heritage are embedded in the cultural and social lives of communities and peoples and form an intrinsic part of their identity. Their resources, contexts, capacities and skill-sets are closely aligned with their cultural landscapes. Therefore, in a changing socio-cultural and economic landscape, their cultural heritage must be taken into account and the process led by the community itself. Through our mapping exercise we saw how communities prioritize certain elements and that helped us look beyond traditional patterns and take into account their contemporary needs, requirements and desires. Another lesson is that the conversations with local women are crucial as they highlight the everyday underlying concerns, such as changing food and health patterns or how certain spaces in the house are more desirable that others because it suits their needs. We observed that women are more concerned with the everyday and that was crucial in understanding what cultural heritage remains relevant for the community today and what are the priorities and associations attached to it.

Mapping the intangible heritage of a particular landscape demands a participatory approach in order to identify, document and analyse the cultural practices and living patterns of a community. By utilizing multiple methods, a range of practices and living patterns are surfaced, which create a platform for local community to revisit and reflect on their cultural landscapes. The LVS participatory model of mapping cultural practices and patterns encourages knowledge exchange between researchers and local communities, where narrative is led by the local community. However, this task poses its own challenges; cultural practices are an intrinsic part of everyday life, hence it is not always easy for community to pronounce these. This is where LVS researchers step in, to observe and document while spending time with men and women in their spaces or taking part in an activity such as picking fruit and drying it, making traditional roti or cooking soup which exemplify how things are done in the everyday life. This documentation is presented to the local community during discursive sessions where they are able to revisit their practices and share more knowledge around these. When the process of documenting the intangible cultural heritage is led by the community, there is greater chance that its protection and preservation will be ensured by the community as they feel a sense of ownership and belonging. Mapping allows the emergence of a narrative that is led by an engaged community who establish and define the historical and contemporary context of their intangible heritage. When this task is conducted by the local community, there is a greater sense of ownership and belonging. Likewise, lessons can be drawn from this mapping exercise for archaeological excavations and intangible cultural heritage protection, especially in developing countries where such projects are often deemed excessive and extravagant. It is about keeping the treasured past relevant for a changing future because that helps communities define who they are and where they belong. In this sense, the mapping project not only produces an inventory of practices but probes a conversation around the possible routes of navigating the changing cultural landscape—what remains relevant, becomes forgotten and what needs to be held on to, improvised and recreated.

REFERENCES

Alexander, C. (1979). *The Timeless Way of Building.* Oxford University Press.

Alexander, C., Ishikawa, S., & Silverstienm, M. (1977). *A Pattern Language: Towns, Buildings, Construction.* New York: Oxford University Press.

Bennett, J. (2012). *Doing Belonging: A Sociological Study of Belonging in Place as the Outcome of Social Practices.* Unpublished Ph.D. Thesis, University of Manchester.

Biagioli, C., & Maria-Olivieri, L. (2014). Conservation and Development: Pakistan Conservation Challenge. In O. Vileikis (Ed.), *The Right to [World] Heritage* (pp. 129–157). Cottbus-Senftenberg: Brandenburgische Technische Universität.

Blake, J. (2009). UNESCO's 2003 Convention on Intangible Cultural Heritage. In L. Smith & N. Akagawa (Eds.), *The Implications of Community Involvement in 'Safeguarding' in Intangible Heritage* (pp. 45–73). London: Routledge.

Cheema, Y. (2007). Towards an Inventory of Historic Buildings and Cultural Landscapes. In S. Bianca (Ed.), *Karakoram: Hidden Treasures in the Northern Areas of Pakistan* (pp. 165–184). Turin: Umberto Allemandi.

Cole, S. (2005). Cultural Tourism, Community Participation and Empowerment in Cultural Tourism in a Changing World. In M. Smith & M. Robinson (Eds.), *Politics, Participation and (Re)presentation* (pp. 89–103). Clevedon: Channel View Publications.

Downs, R., & Stea, D. (Eds.). (1974). *Image and Environment: Cognitive Mapping and Spatial Behaviour.* New York: Hodder & Stoughton.

Grasseni, C. (Ed.). (2012). Community Mapping as Auto-Ethno-Cartography. In *Advances in Visual Methodology* (pp. 97–112). London: Sage.

Ingold, T. (1993). The Temporality of the Landscape. *World Archaeology, 25*(2), 152–174.

Ingold, T. (2000). *The Perception of the Environment Essays on Livelihood, Dwelling and Skill.* London: Routledge.

Jigyasu, R. (2016). Reducing Disaster Risks to Urban Cultural Heritage: Global Challenges and Opportunities. *Journal of Heritage Management, 1*(1), 59–67.

Kesby, M. (2000). Participatory Diagramming: Deploying Qualitative Methods Through an Action Research Epistemology. *Area, 32*(4), 423–435.

Kindon, S. (2010). Participation. In S. Smith, R. Pain, S. Marston, & J. Jones (Eds.), *The Sage Handbook of Social Geographies* (pp. 517–545). London: Sage.

Kitchin, R. (1994). Cognitive Maps: What Are They and Why Study Them? *Journal of Environmental Psychology, 14*(1), 1–19.

Kovach, M. (2009). *Indigenous Methodologies: Characteristics, Conversations and Contexts.* Toronto: University of Toronto Press.

Kurin, R. (2007). Safeguarding Intangible Cultural Heritage: Key Factors in Implementing the 2003 Convention. *International Journal of Intangible Heritage, 2,* 9–20.

Munjeri, D. (2009). Following the Length and Breadth of the Roots: Some Dimensions of Intangible Heritage. In L. Smith & N. Akagawa (Eds.), *Intangible Heritage* (pp. 131–150). London: Routledge.

Oliver-Smith, A. (2006). The Centrality of Culture in Post-Disaster Reconstruction. *Prince Claus Fund Journal, 14,* 20–29.

Peers, L., & Brown, A. K. (2007). Museums and Source Communities. In S. Watson (Ed.), *Museums and Their Communities* (pp. 519–537). London: Routledge.

Rose, M. (2002). Landscape and Labyrinths. *Geoforum, 33,* 455–467.

Salingaros, N. A. (2006). *A Theory of Architecture.* Solingen: Umbau-Verlag.

Seitel, P. (2001). Proceedings of Smithsonian-UNESCO Conference Forthcoming. *Smithsonian Talk Story, 20,* 13.

Smith, L., & Waterton, E. (2009). *Heritage, Communities and Archaeology.* London: Duckworth.

Stevens, P. (2012). Towards an Ecosociology. *Sociology, 46,* 579–595.

Taylor, K., & Lennon, J. (2011). Cultural Landscapes: A Bridge Between Culture and Nature? *International Journal of Heritage Studies, 17*(6), 537–554.

Thompson, J. (2008). Hede kehe'hotzi'kahidi': My Journey to a Tahlatan Research Paradigm. *Canadian Journal of Native Education, 31*(1), 24–39.

Waterton, E., & Smith, L. (2010). The Recognition and Misrecognition of Community Heritage. *International Journal of Heritage Studies, 16*(1–2), 4–15.

Watson, S. (Ed.). (2007). *Museums and Their Communities.* London: Routledge.

CHAPTER 9

Community Engagement in Natural Heritage Conservation Stewardship, Nepal

Rajendra Narsingh Suwal

Abstract Suwal highlights damaging factors linked to the nationalization of forests in Nepal that coincided with the campaign to eradicate malaria in the Terai from the mid-1950s onwards and with the colonizing of areas of low population to increase agricultural production. As a result there was a loss of natural habitat that threatened plant and wildlife. Recognizing the danger, the government initiated programmes that established protected areas and buffer zones and community forest stewardship as self-sustaining mechanisms. Suwal argues that well-planned community engagement processes, linked to longer term local economic benefits, encouraged people to support and engage in natural heritage protection. Suwal notes the positive role NGOs, such as the World Wildlife Fund, have played in supporting community in activities such as community stewardship and eco-tourism.

Keywords Nepal · Community forest stewardship · Legislation

R. N. Suwal (✉)
WWF Nepal, Kathmandu, Nepal
e-mail: rajendra.suwal@wwfnepal.org

© The Author(s) 2019
R. Coningham and N. Lewer (eds.), *Archaeology, Cultural Heritage Protection and Community Engagement in South Asia*,
https://doi.org/10.1007/978-981-13-6237-8_9

9.1   Introduction

Nepal has achieved a notable transition in natural heritage conservation, changing from strict protection to a participatory and revenue-sharing mechanism. In the past, the combination of an under-resourced government and poor communities meant that preventing encroachment of forests and plundering of resources was difficult. This chapter will review the new legislation that allowed and promoted ethical protection and conservation of natural heritage in Nepal, and give examples of community forestry and people engagement in these approaches, especially in the development of community-led forest eco-tourism that directly benefits the economy and the local population.

9.2   Legislation

9.2.1   Forest Destruction

Paudel (2002) and Subedi et al. (2014) describe in some detail the history behind the tragedy of earlier deforestation in Nepal. Key landmarks were the 1957 Private Forest Nationalization Act and the 1961 Forest Act, both enacted following the abolition of the Rana Regime in 1950 (Nepal Law Commission 2015). The basic premise of the two Acts was that forests were the property of the state and, as Paudel (2002) noted, were to be rapidly exploited to supply much needed national timber, fuel energy and other forest products, so increasing state revenue. These legal instruments overlapped with the campaign to eradicate malaria in the Terai from the mid-1950s onwards, a key step in colonizing low populated areas and expanding agriculture production. Unfortunately, these legal processes led to many individuals perceiving forests as the sole jurisdiction and responsibility of the state. This also led to the reclassification of those living in newly nationalized forests as "squatters", a terminology still applied today, and thus established a challenging forest governance legacy.

9.2.2   Modern Approaches

In 1959 the naturalist Edward Pritchard Gee, of the Flora and Fauna Society and IUCN, made an exploratory visit to survey rhino and other wildlife in Chitwan. His findings warned the Government about the dire situation of Nepal's wildlife. The government responded quickly and designated the Mahendra Deer Mriga Kunj (Mahendra Deer Park) in 1959 along the Tikaluli Barandabhar Forest bordering the Rapti River in the south. They also set up the Rhino Sanctuary south of the Rapti River in Chitwan, while the Armed Rhino Patrol was started in 1963. These were followed by the declaration of Chitwan as Nepal's first National Park and the promulgation of 1973 National Parks and Wildlife Conservation Act. The Nepal Army has been assigned to protect the core areas of National Parks and Wildlife Reserves since 1975, while the Armed Rhino Patrol now protects rhino and wildlife outside the boundaries of the National Parks (CNP 2015). The Chitwan National Park was inscribed on the list of World Heritage Sites by UNESCO in 1984 (Fig. 9.1).

The success behind the protected area management of Nepal may be credited to the Government's response to public demands, backed by scientific knowledge and legislative provisions. This is the basis for the sustainability of local initiatives in the ownership of natural areas, and is supported by a number of legislative opportunities for people's

Fig. 9.1 One-horned Rhino in Nepal's Chitwan

participation in the conservation and management of natural resources. For example, the 1996 Conservation Area Management Regulation empowered local communities to become directly engaged in natural heritage stewardship and management (DNPWC 2013).

9.3   NATIONAL PARKS AND WILDLIFE CONSERVATION

Over the years, there have been a number of legislative provisions that have established and promoted a meaningful engagement for communities in natural heritage regeneration, conservation and protection. These include the 1973 National Parks and Wildlife Conservation Act (4th amendment, 1993), which allowed the Government of Nepal (GoN) to establish Protected Areas (PAs), such as National Parks (NPs), Wildlife Reserves (WRs), Hunting Reserves (HRs), Conservation Areas (CAs) and Buffer Zones (BZs) in any part of the country through a gazette notification for conservation of flora and fauna. It also recognized economic development as core by legal provision to grant permission to establish hotels/lodges, rafting camping sites and other such businesses by granting permission and permission for licensed hunting in designated hunting reserves (HR). Significantly, it promoted community involvement in conservation by allowing the PAs to spend between 30 and 50% of revenues generated in the PAs on community development in coordination with local government (http://www.dnpwc.gov.np/).

The Department of National Parks and Wildlife Conservation (DNPWC) was established in 1980 with the responsibility conserving Nepal's wildlife and outstanding landscapes of ecological importance for the well-being of its people. The primary objectives of the DNPWC are to conserve important ecosystems, unique natural and cultural heritage and give protection to valuable and endangered wildlife species. Key activities include habitat management, species conservation, anti-poaching operations, conservation education and eco-tourism promotion in and around the protected area system (http://www.dnpwc.gov.np/).

A total of 23.39% of Nepal's area is currently under PAs with twelve NPs, one WR, one HR, six CAs and 13 BZs (Table 9.1; Fig. 9.2). There are about 546 functioning Buffer Zone Community Forests with 94,626 households as members (Bower et al. 2017). The 1993 Forest Act authorized the GoN, and appropriate authorities, to undertake activities which provide a strong base for (eco-)tourism through the conservation

Table 9.1 Protected wildlife and conservation area types and area coverage in Nepal

Protected area type	No.	Total area (square kilometress)
National Park (NP)	12	11,806.02
Wildlife Reserve (WR)	1	175
Hunting Reserve (HR)	1	1325
Conservation Area (CA)	6	15,425.95
Buffer Zone (BZ)	13	5687.78
Total	33	34,419.75

of forest and forest resources, conservation of wetlands, conservation of national forests and handing over a forest to become a Community Forest. Its legislation also allows the conservation and sustainable use of non-timber forest products (NTFPs) as well as the declaration and conservation of special areas as protected forests (http://dof.gov.np/).

The 2000 Conservation Area Management Regulations is another critical instrument as it offers detailed criteria for Conservation Areas (CAs) and governs the systems and processes for their establishment. It can designate the management of CAs through either government or non-government agencies and its regulations state that related Village Development Committee (VDC) must form a Conservation Area Management Committee (CAMC) to conduct community development related construction work, protect the natural environment and offer effective implementation of the management plan. The CAMC also needs to prepare a management plan to implement eco-tourism development and conservation of natural/cultural heritage (http://www.dnpwc.gov.np/).

9.4   BUFFER ZONES

The 1996 Management Regulation and Buffer Zone Management Guidelines further empowered community leaders by allowing them to become elected Chairmen with Chief Wardens as ex-officio Member Secretary. Buffer Zone User Committee (BZUC) members are also now democratically elected from the community forest Buffer Zone User Group (BZUG) members, specifically including representation of

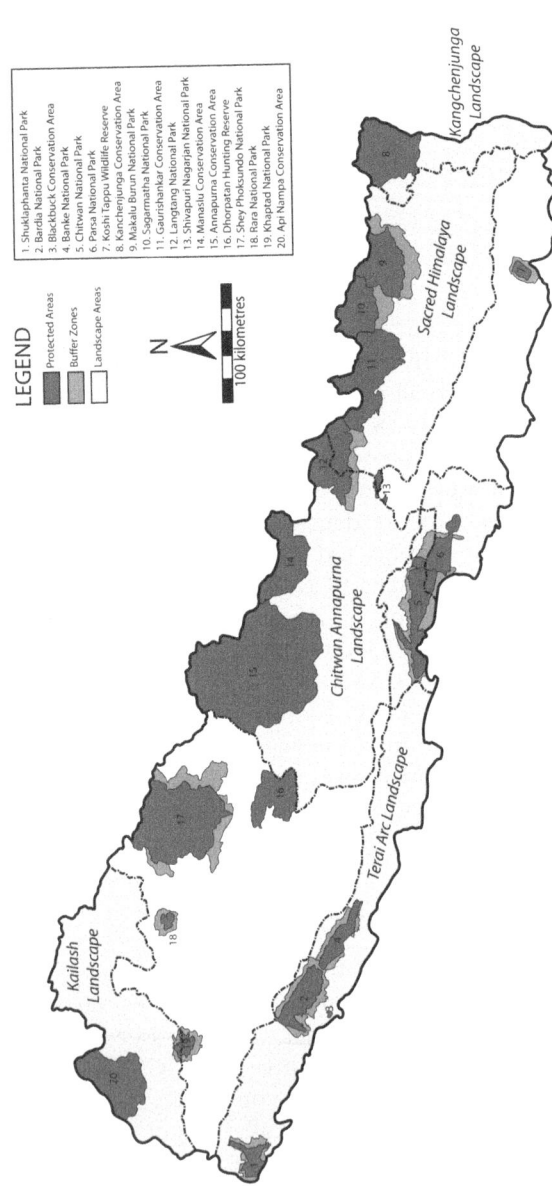

Fig. 9.2   Map of National Parks, Wildlife Reserves, Hunting Reserves, Conservation Areas and Buffer Zones in Nepal

women and marginalized communities. Elements of the Buffer Zone Management Rules (BZMR) and Directives (1996) include the framework within which the Buffer Zones will be established and managed. It grants the PA manager the right to establish the network of BZUGs and BZUCs with the Buffer Zone Management Committee (BZMC) as the apex body. The guidelines advocate the preparation of a five-year BZ Management Plan, which includes activities for tourism development, soil and environment conservation and preservation of cultural and historical heritage. Finally, the regulations regarding the fund usage are restrictive, whereby the following budget headings must be allocated set percentages of the funds: conservation 30%, community development 30%, income generation and skill development 20%, conservation education 10%, with administrative costs at only 10% (http://www.dnpwc.gov.np/).

Clearly, the buffer zone institutions at different levels aim to make communities self-reliant by involving them in implementation of the various programmes and capacity building activities. The programme has been successful particularly in natural resource conservation, social mobilization, development of alternative energy and human resource development at community levels. The mainstreaming of special target groups and women to ensure their fair representation in the buffer zone institutions and maintaining group cohesiveness is an emerging challenge for management and constant support is required to change the attitude and perception of people in conservation. It is increasingly recognized that there is a need to adopt a strategy for a development plan in each protected area which is pro-poor, pro-women and pro-special target groups (Maskey and Bajimaya 2005: 3).

9.5 Community Forests

Community forestry has been defined as "the control, protection and management of forest resources by rural communities for whom trees and forests are an integral part of their farming systems" (Gilmour and Fisher 1991: 8). While Joshi (2003) noted some early challenges with community forestry, as will be shown, there have been considerable benefits. Anticipated impacts of community forests are the restoration of degraded forests, resumed greenery, increased biodiversity, increased supply of forest products, empowered women, poor and disadvantaged

groups, increased income generation and improved livelihood (dof.gov.
np).

As is clear, the legislation accepts and promotes community engagement in planning and management as a vital tool that:

- enables and improves the capacity of local people to manage resources sustainably;
- improves the environment—forest, soil, water, etc.;
- increases local awareness concerning environmental and social problems;
- promotes biodiversity conservation efforts;
- strengthens local culture and heritage conservation efforts;
- generates substantial revenues for community development;
- and gathers information based on research that contributes to drafting and endorsing acts/regulations (dof.gov.np).

The objective of the 1978 Community Forest Programme (CFP) was to achieve sustainable management of forest resources by converting accessible forests into community forests in a phased process. This has been met with the result that 1.45 million households, or 35% of the population of Nepal, is currently involved in a community forestry management programme. To date 19,361 Community Forest Units (CFUs) have been formed with 1072 women as committee members, a total of 1,813,478 hectares of National Forest have been handed over as community forests, and 24,661,549 people have benefitted (dof.gov.np). The next section will give examples of community stewardship projects.

9.5.1   Baghmara Community Forest Stewardship and Buffer Zones

The concept for a buffer zone plantation programme was developed by the Nepal Conservation Research and Training Centre of the then King Mahendra Trust Fund for Nature Conservation in 1989. The programme's main objective was to:

> increase habitat for the endangered wildlife while providing fodder, fuelwood and timber for the local people. Furthermore, by opening the community forest area for eco-tourism, the project aimed to demonstrate to the local people the economic value of conservation. The project was launched in the Baghmara Forest of the Bachhauli Village Development Committee (VDC) on the north-east boundary of the park, an area that

had become degraded and overgrazed due to a lack of attention from government authorities and increasing needs of the local people. The Department of National Parks and Wildlife Conservation helped the project by providing technical assistance and materials for the plantations. (https://sustainabledevelopment.un.org/content/dsd/dsd_aofw_mg/mg_success_stories/csd7/tour9.htm)

At the initiation of the local community in Sauraha, the Baghmara Forest (meaning "Tiger Hunt"), with support from WWF, and leadership provided by the National Trust for Nature Conservation and the GoN, was declared a community forest in 1989. The forest was home to wide biodiversity including the Bengal tiger, crocodile, deer, one-horned rhinoceros and a plethora of different species of insects, flowers and trees. All were in danger from encroachment and illegal poaching, and public grazing areas were occupied by illegal land dealers. Through the programme, the community was given the authority to manage the forest in 1995. Three decades later, this restored CF has become a refuge for threatened animals and has helped to reduce the tourism pressure from the core area of the national park. Community development and economy has also benefitted from schemes such as bio-gas plants, toilet constructions, employment related to tourism and loans to start microenterprises.

Learning from the Baghmara Community Forest in Chitwan helped guide the development of Buffer Zone Management Rules in 1996 for people living adjacent to protected areas. It was seen to empower the communities with a provision for revenue generation, including eco-tourism, while protecting the forest and endangered wildlife. As noted by the UN's Department of Economic and Social Affairs, the Baghmara Community Forest project has become a model of sustainable community forest conservation and attracts national and international visitors to learn from their experience (https://sustainabledevelopment.un.org/content/dsd/dsd_aofw_mg/mg_success_stories/csd7/tour9.htm).

9.5.2 *Annapurna Conservation Area*

The establishment of the Annapurna Conservation Area in 1986 also meant that the community had direct involvement during management and decision processes (www.ntnc.org.np/project/annapurna-conservation-area-project) and also retained the ownership of private property. It is a non-militarized protected area system of Nepal; the first of its kind, and WWF was instrumental in supporting the government in designing this programme (Heinen and Kattel 1992). Believed to attract more than 60% of international tourists to Nepal, the Area's 762,900 hectares support over 1000 tea shops and lodges (NTNC 2013). The fee for foreigners is 3000 Nepali Rupees per entry +13% VAT and 1000 Nepali Rupees per entry + 13% VAT for SAARC nationals and 100 NPR for Nepali nationals   (https://www.welcomenepal.com/plan-your-trip/park-entry-fees.html). All the revenue earned by Annapurna Conservation Area Project (ACAP) is spent on resident communities to meet basic needs such as education, health, alternative energy and trekking trails, including conservation.

9.5.3   Kangchenjungha Conservation Area

The Kanchenjunga Conservation Area (KCA) was the GoN's "gift to the earth" in 1997 and a Kanchenjunga Conservation Area Management Council (KCAMC) was formed with support from WWF Nepal in April 2003. It consisted of seven Conservation Area User Committees, forty-four User Groups, and thirty-two Mother Groups. Community forest user group composition required democratically elected members, including women, marginalized community and socially discarded strata of society to be represented in all planning and decision-making processes. There is also a need for constant support to change the attitude, perception, governance, transparency, accountability and deliverables.

The KCAMC was the first community to receive the management authority of a CA from the GoN in 2006, since when it has been successfully managed for nearly a decade with support from the government and WWF Nepal. The "capacitated" citizen scientists of Kanchenjunga have assisted the government in snow leopard research, blue sheep monitoring and conservation stewardship. The clearest indicator of the success of this project is the revival of over two dozen snow leopards roaming these alpine habitats within two decades of conservation effort (WWF 2018). The way forward for KCAMC's sustainability is also to promote high value and low volume tourism.

The KCA is proof that when communities are empowered to manage their resources, provided with livelihood options linked to biodiversity, and when good governance practices are institutionalized, they are very likely to become conservation stewards (WWF Nepal 2018). Clearly, such a community-based management strategy might well be applicable for conservation stewardship of many other cultural and archaeological heritage sites of Nepal.

9.5.3.1 Lessons Learned from KCAMC

WWF Nepal (2018) has identified a number of lessons learned from the KCAMC programme, centrally, that the handover of KCA to the KCAMC increased local ownership and with it instilled a greater sense of responsibility and stewardship. Local institutions and capacities are crucial to sustain conservation programmes. WWF Nepal also noted that improved understanding of the community's new roles and responsibilities as conservation stewards, and rights to natural resource governance to landscape-scales had to be overcome through a series of community workshops, training programmes, orientations and study tours.

As remote mountain communities face many livelihood and infrastructure challenges, conservation interventions must address these to ensure communities see the value in engagement. Value-added market linkages also maximized the economic revenues returning to local communities, encouraging establishment of microenterprises and entrepreneurship. Participatory mapping exercises using Climate Vulnerability and Capacity Analysis (CVCA) methods enabled communities to understand vulnerabilities and adaptation techniques and demonstrated that citizen scientists in the KCA can conduct blue sheep census independently and snow leopard camera trap monitoring with minimum input from the experts.

Despite engagement, we also found that most communities will tolerate a certain degree of conflict but that proactive conflict mitigation strategies are essential to prevent its escalation beyond the threshold of tolerance. The innovative community-managed livestock insurance scheme contributed immensely towards overcoming human–wildlife conflict. Finally, it was recognized that long-term investment of between 10 and 15 years was required to implement phase wise conservation and development interventions for sustainability.

9.5.3.2 The Way Forward for KCAMC

WWF Nepal (2018) also formulated approaches and strategies to further build KCAMC based on the need to further capacitate the community as an ongoing effort for their development of governance skills, financial planning, transparency and monitoring mechanism. The following strategies were also recommended for continuation and upscaling in KCA, as well as their replication in other landscapes:

- Community-based species monitoring through citizen scientists. Currently, the focus is only on the snow leopard and its prey base. It should be extended to other species such as red panda, musk deer and threatened avifauna.
- Community managed livestock insurance schemes. The four schemes currently managed by the communities are effectively run. It is now practised only for livestock killings by snow leopards. It needs to be continued and its scope increased to other animals such as the wolf, wild dog, common leopard and others.
- Community-based anti-poaching operations engaging youth in conservation has worked well and there is a need to continue increasing monitoring/patrolling frequencies in poaching sensitive areas.
- Gender and social inclusion. KCAMC institutions are ensured with at least 33% of women representation in council and committees empowering women through mothers' groups.
- Sustainable financing and self-sustenance. Programmes to seek sustainable funds and to make the KCA self-sustaining must be pursued—Non Timber Forest Products (NTFP), tourism, sustainable harvesting of blue sheep, and streamlining community capitals into cooperatives and microfinance institutions.
- A Tri-nation peace park was envisioned to increase collaboration between neighbours China, India and Nepal.

9.5.4   Amaltari Homestays—Living with the Community

WWF Nepal's homestay programme was initiated in 2011 in Dalla, a village adjoining the Bardia National Park Buffer Zone. Currently sixteen WWF Nepal supported community-based homestays are in operation in the Terai Arc Landscape. The primary objective of the livelihood support is to provide conservation benefits while encouraging community stewardship in conservation. The Amaltari Homestay programme

Fig. 9.3 Amaltari community homestays

is located in the buffer zone of Chitwan National Park in Nawalparasi District, with more than 200 households from several indigenous communities. It was established in 2013 and within five years became the leading homestay in the network. It is a part of WWF Nepal's Sustainable Communities Initiative (SCI) based on three pillars: environmental safeguard, economic benefit and social justice. According to a survey report, the key motivations to start a community-based homestay in Amaltari was to improve the income of the family (47.6%) followed by utilizing time for constructive work, and conservation of nature (9.5%) (Karki 2016).

Amaltari homestay facilities have 24 households with 48 twin rooms and 96 beds. Ancillary services and enterprises include jeep and elephant safaris, a cultural centre, cultural dances and a handicraft shop. The net earnings of the Amaltari homestay initiative to date (2019) is about $350,000 by hosting over 53,000 guests (Fig. 9.3). The National Park Authority is also considering whether to permit the BZUCs to build and operate accommodated watchtowers in the buffer areas to promote further eco-tourism (personal communication with Dhani Ram Mahato, Chairman, Amaltari Homestay Committee). This could be a great opportunity forward for a low volume and high revenue tourism economy if they strategize the provision thoughtfully. Homestays have also been found to encourage youths to become members of the Community Based Antipoaching Units (CBAPUs). As in other cases, CBAPU's are the first line of sharing information with park personnel. Other initiatives taken by the community include grassland/wetland habitat management, forest restoration and vulture conservation.

9.6   Conclusion

From the examples given in this chapter, we can draw a number of lessons learned for good practice when thinking about community engagement in natural heritage conservation stewardship in Nepal. These can, and do, inform the development and management of community forests more widely. Enabling conditions are made if a neutral catalyst such as WWF Nepal brings the stakeholders to a common forum to discuss the situation, demands, required legal provisions, and technology and resources needed. Firstly, it is clear that success depends on a supportive government; through acts and regulations, as the legal provision shared with the community has encouraged conservation stewardship. Dialogue for concessional policy in the buffer zone with government and linking markets has also been an opportunity for the development of low volume high value eco-tourism.

Secondly, it is clear that a motivated and proactive community is required to support government legislation, and that co-operation and collaboration between government and non-government sectors act as a multiplying factor in community motivation. This, in turn, includes improvement in health, education, economic development and employment sectors. Thirdly, we recognize that communities need long-term support and assistance in planning and designing conservation strategies and managed tourism development. This may require additional capacity building such as access to hospitality skills, access to finance and market linkage and quality control.

In conclusion, well-planned community engagement and mobilization processes that are linked to economic benefits, led people to support natural heritage protection as they come to acknowledge and value the long-term benefits that come from protecting and conserving forests rather than short-term economic gains.

N.B. The contents in this chapter are the responsibility of the author and do not necessarily reflect the views of WWF Nepal.

REFERENCES

Bower, J., Dickerson, A., & Yuan, Q. (2017). *Buffer Zone Planning Nepal's Shivapuri Nagarjung National Park: Inclusive Program Development for More Resilient Park People Relation and the Protection of Ecological Services in Kathmandu.* Unpublished Master's Thesis, University of Michigan.

CNP. (2015). *Chitwan National Park and Its Buffer Zone Management Plan 2013–2017.* Chitwan: Government of Nepal, Ministry of Forest and Soil Conservation.

DNPWC. (2013). *Chitwan National Park and Its Buffer Zone: Management Plan (2013–2017).* Kathmandu: DNPWC.

Gilmour, D. A., & Fisher, R. J. (1991). *Villagers, Forests and Foresters—the Philosophy, Process and Practice of Community Forestry in Nepal.* Kathmandu: Sahayogi Press.

Heinen, T., & Kattel, B. (1992). Parks, People, and Conservation: A Review of Management Issues in Nepal's Protected Areas. *Population and Environment, 14*(1), 49–84.

Joshi, M. (2003). *Community Forestry Programs in Nepal and Their Effects on Poorer Households.* Paper Presented at the XII World Forestry Congress, Quebec City, Canada.

Karki, K. (2016). *Assessment of Homestay Program at Amaltari Village of Nawalparasi, Nepal.* Unpublished BSc Thesis, Tribhuvan University.

Maskey, T., & Bajimaya, S. (2005). Participatory Management of Buffer Zone for Natural Resources Conservation in Nepal. *Banko Janakari, 15*(1), 3–10.

Nepal Law Commission. (2015). https://www.lawcommission.gov.np/en/documents/2015/08/private-forests-nationalization-act-2013-1957.pdf.

Paudel, S. (2002). Community Forest in Nepal. *Himalayan Journal of Sciences, 1*(1), 62–65.

Subedi, B. P., Ghimire, P. L., Koontz, A., Khanal, S. C., Katwal, S. C., Sthapit, K. R., & Khadka Mishra, S. (2014). *Private Sector Involvement and Investment in Nepal's Forestry: Status, Prospects and Ways Forward. Study Report.* Kathmandu: Multi-Stakeholder Forestry Programme Services Support Unit.

WWF Nepal. (2018). *Kanchenjunga Conservation Area: A Retrospective Report 2018.* Kathmandu: WWF.

CHAPTER 10

Reclaiming the Heritage of Bagan: Communities in Myanmar Learn to Raise Their Voice

Kai Weise

Abstract Bagan is one of the most important religious sites in Myanmar. However, over the past decades, local communities have not been allowed to partake in its management. Weise describes the challenges of managing Bagan, particularly after the 2016 Chauk Earthquake and provides insight into the process of nominating Bagan for World Heritage status during the transition of the Myanmar Government through democratic elections. These changes have allowed local communities to raise their voices against continued mismanagement and the lack of local governance. Weise concludes that for living cultural heritage sites to be sustainable, communities need to be allowed to participate by expressing themselves within a context of safety and stability, thus helping to ensure cultural continuity.

Keywords Myanmar · Bagan · Community · Heritage protection

K. Weise (✉)
International Council on Monuments and Sites (ICOMOS),
Kathmandu, Nepal

© The Author(s) 2019
R. Coningham and N. Lewer (eds.), *Archaeology, Cultural Heritage Protection and Community Engagement in South Asia*,
https://doi.org/10.1007/978-981-13-6237-8_10

137

10.1   INTRODUCTION: BAGAN, AN ANCIENT SITE
WITH CONTINUED SIGNIFICANCE

Tucked into the bend of the Ayeyarwady River in the central dry zone of Myanmar, sits a landscape comprising of over 3000 ancient monuments scattered across a huge area predominantly of farmland (Fig. 10.1). The monuments, largely neglected by state authorities, were maintained over the decades by local Buddhist communities who collected contributions to rebuild them, allowing donors to gain merit. This changed after an earthquake hit Bagan in 1975 damaging many sites, after which the international community provided support for restoration and initiated the nomination of Bagan for World Heritage status. This was deferred by the World Heritage Committee (WHC) in 1997, who requested further information but the government considered this a rejection and clamped down on foreign involvement in Bagan.

The communities in Myanmar had little to say during military rule and dissent could be dealt with harshly. In 1990 communities were

Fig. 10.1   Traditional farming practised between the temples and shrines of Bagan

displaced from around the ruins of Old Bagan and were given little support to build their new homes. The trauma that they experienced still runs deep in their psyche and defines their opinion of the government. However, between 1995 and 2011, influential individuals were given free rein to build hotels and resorts within the archaeological area. This changed slowly with liberalization in 2011 and the establishment of a transitional government. The process of nominating Bagan for World Heritage was resurrected and the election in November 2015, won by Daw Aung San Suu Kyi's party, meant changes to the system of governance. However, with the Army still holding key ministries such as Home Affairs and Defence, it was a difficult relationship that ensued. While the Regional Government was led by the democratically elected party, local governance and the District Administrator were still controlled by the Army.

This chapter provides an introduction to Bagan as a potential World Heritage site and the challenges faced while establishing a management system. Furthermore, the position of the community in this critical phase of political transformation and in the process of preparing the World Heritage nomination dossier will be explored. After the Chauk Earthquake that damaged monuments in August 2016, State Councillor Daw Aung San Suu Kyi visited Bagan. Discussing ongoing nomination processes for World Heritage status, she stated that the management of Bagan must not only deal with conserving the monuments but must also consider community needs and engagement.

10.2   Historic Disruptions and Continuity: From the Pyu Through the Bagan Period to Colonial Rule

The earlier history of Bagan is shrouded in legend. There was some building activity around Bagan during the Pyu Period that lasted till the mid-ninth century CE that would have included the earliest walls and most of 'Old Bagan'. Folklore records that there were 19 original villages in the area and five early palace sites, but little has been excavated. It was between the eleventh and thirteenth centuries that Bagan developed into the capital of an empire. King Anawratha, who ruled Bagan between 1044 and 1077 CE, built a palace within the ancient city walls. This was partially excavated in 2003, exposing a sprawling complex of which we only have a glimpse of its full grandeur. To the east are the remains of the later palace built by King Kyansittha who reigned between 1084 and 1113 CE. The palaces are said to have been of wood with roofs gilded with pure gold but were all ravaged by fires (Weise 2013).

Bagan has over 3000 monuments, comprising temples, stupas, monasteries, ordination halls, caves and unexcavated mounds scattered over an area of a hundred square kilometres. The fervour of building these religious structures began under the patronage of King Anawratha who, according to legends, conquered Thaton to bring back copies of the Tipitaka and embrace Theravada teachings. However, the art and architecture of Bagan still retained a diverse set of themes ranging from local pre-Buddhist beliefs to the pantheon of Mahayana Buddhism and even drawing on inspiration from Hinduism (Weise 2014). Most of these buildings were completed during this golden age, which lasted for two and a half centuries.

Kublai Khan's Mongol forces repeatedly attacked the kingdom in the late thirteenth century, leading to the decline and abandonment of the city. Due to this, and also general internal discord, King Narathihapati fled Bagan in 1287 CE (Weise 2013). The remains of this expansive city are mostly brick monuments or mounds left after destruction caused by recurring earthquakes. Parts of the fortification walls that were laid out as a square around Old Bagan have been washed away by the Ayeyarwady. There are no remains of the habitations of the common people, whose houses must have been constructed of perishable materials. Even though the golden age of Bagan is known to have ended in the thirteenth century, it is possible to trace cultural continuity in the following centuries through religious activities such as festivals and rituals that continued at many of the temples and pagodas. Numerous temples were also added and embellished with a new style of mural paintings.

So, although the imperial status of Bagan was lost, the local culture associated with the monuments such as festivals and rituals persisted. Today, this historic landscape lies between the towns of Nyaung U and New Bagan (Fig. 10.2). There is development pressure related to the growing number of tourists visiting the site, and the changing socioeconomic conditions of the local population are impacting the towns and villages. There is also a clear threat that the agricultural land around the monuments will either be abandoned or commercially farmed (Weise 2015b: 97–102).

Fig. 10.2 Plan of the archaeological site of Bagan

Urban Area / Village

Buffer Zone

Nominated Property Area

N

1 kilometre

Nyaung U

Ayeyarwady River

Old Bagan

New Bagan

10.3   Challenges of Managing Bagan: Earthquakes and an Elusive World Heritage Status

While Bagan has gone through tumultuous political and natural events, many of the monumental religious structures remain. There is evidence of restoration work carried out even after the fall of the Bagan Empire in the fourteenth century CE. This was followed by a construction spree during the Konbaung Period in the eighteenth and nineteenth centuries. (MORAC/GOM 2018, Vol. 1: 139). However, it seems that religious structures were prioritized and hardly any evidence of other components of the Bagan metropolis remains. The subsurface archaeology of some palaces have been excavated but very little is known of the settlement itself.

An archaeological survey of Burma was established in 1934 during British rule but, prior to this, some attempts were made by the Archaeological Survey of India to study Bagan's monuments. However, these were restricted mainly to identifying archaeological sites and structures were left to deteriorate. A German visitor removed mural paintings from several temples, demonstratively leaving behind his signature and date, supposedly in protest of this neglect. It was only after Independence, and the establishment of the Department of Archaeology in 1954, that more detailed inventories were prepared.

The earthquake that struck Bagan on 8th July 1975 caused extensive damage, mainly through the collapse of elements such as towers and turrets. The two-decade long campaign to restore and conserve the monuments brought some beneficial results but it was a project that did not engage the local community. Highly technical solutions were introduced, initially using reinforced cement concrete, and later prioritizing steel ties and caging methods (Gavrilovic et al. 2016). Concrete, mainly in the form of ring beams, was introduced hidden behind brickwork. Structures were also tied together using steel rods that were inserted and grouted in place with concrete (Gavrilovic 1992). Additionally, extensive research was carried out on the mural paintings followed by consolidation and cleaning of these masterpieces (Lunsford 2012).

The post-earthquake restoration was well under way by the 1990s when more ambitious plans were contrived. An inventory of all monuments was prepared by Pierre Pichard that was later published by UNESCO (Pichard 1992–2001) and a master plan for the preservation of the historic area of Bagan was prepared by a UNESCO team under Professor Yukio Nishimura between 1994 and 1996 (Nishimura 1996).

An inventory, prepared in 1997 with Japanese support, placed selected monuments under three categories: Grade One had 34 monuments, Grade Two 100 monuments and Grade Three 288 monuments. As per the former Deputy Director-General U Aung Kyaing, the parameters for these categories were linked to the assessment of the quality and state of the mural paintings, the architecture and the stucco ornamentation. This was part of the overall effort in preparing Bagan for inclusion on the list of World Heritage. For the first attempt, a nomination dossier was prepared in 1994 and submitted in 1995. However, a newly defined process required Bagan to be first inscribed on the Tentative List for World Heritage, which was done in 1996.

At the WHC session in 1997, the consideration of Bagan was based on the evaluation report and recommendations prepared by ICOMOS (ICOMOS 1997). The main concerns were the lack of management to ensure the site's protection and uncertainty concerning the boundaries as the Master Plan had not yet been finalized and adopted. The nomination focused on the monuments, however, there was a concern in respect to some of the restoration works that were being listed. A referral acknowledges the submitted nomination as still valid and only required the State Party to submit additional information. This would have needed to be done within three years but, while a revised draft nomination dossier was prepared in 2000, this was never submitted.

The WHC had concerns about inappropriate development activities, including the construction of a golf course, the widening of a road crossing the heritage site and a substantive museum within the archaeological site of Old Bagan. Other controversial projects included the building of hotels in the heritage area, especially within and next to the walled city. This was closely linked to the inappropriate sale of land to private national and international developers. There were facilities constructed near Anawrahta's Palace, such as an observation tower and a religious research centre (Pichard 2012) and there was also a worry about the expansion of towns and villages leading to encroachment beyond settlement boundaries.

In 1995 a collection of national and international funds for reconstruction of temples and stupas on the archaeological mounds was started. This reconstruction of several hundred temples and pagodas on archaeological mounds, based on a catalogue of assumed designs, has become a main concern in respect to loss of authenticity. As noted on a signboard near the museum, there were 1175 monuments that had been renovated (with a further 700 remaining) and new constructions on 689 brick mounds (with a further 203 remaining) between 1995 and 2005. The first category would include the restoration of spires, vaults or walls. The second category would have consisted of clearing the brick mounds, identifying the foundations and rebuilding the structure on top of these. Also new monuments had been added where there were no ancient plinths, causing confusion when new inventories were being prepared and when these were compared to older versions. We still are not sure how many monuments there are in Bagan, with the official number recently being changed from 3122 to 3595 monuments.

The reconstruction of monuments on original plinths has been justified as a continuation of a tradition that was the basis for the initial creation of Bagan itself. Merit-making through building and restoring religious structures has been the core motivation for building and maintaining these monuments. Questionable, however, might be the means, and particularly the quality, of the new construction which was carried out using cement mortar to recreate the external form of the structure with infill being done using ancient bricks. Donors could choose their projects based on size and budget, and building was carried out by private contractors. Some drawings exist but there is no documentation for most of these poorly built structures, evidence of which became apparent when many were damaged by the heavy rains during the monsoon of 2015 (Weise 2015a).

Experts working on the World Heritage nomination of Bagan decided that whilst the reconstruction of new monuments on ancient archaeological plinths might be justified, it should not be continued. However, there were more complex issues that the new site management had to deal with which lay much closer to the hearts of the communities. Dealing with living heritage has become a critical part of managing sites like Bagan. For example, the gilding of Dhamma-yazika Pagoda was initially questioned by the Department of Archaeology and conservation experts. The involvement of communities in the post-earthquake response of 2016 offered both a challenge and an opportunity for the beneficial long-term management of Bagan. Critical here is differentiating between community activities and external speculators and developers (Weise 2015b).

10.4 Community Engagement After Decades of Silence

In 1990 people living in Old Bagan were relocated south to New Bagan. The main reason was that they had been tunnelling their way into the archaeology of the palace sites looking for gold from the roofs of the gutted ancient palaces. In addition, the inhabitants of Nyaung U and Myinkabar, ancient villages from the Pyu Period, did not want the relocated people to live near what they perceived as their more respectable and ancient communities. New Bagan, also known as Bagan Myothit, was therefore planned further south but this was unfortunately built partially on even earlier archaeological palace sites. To the north-east was the Kyaunk Saga palace site, founded in the second century CE by King Tha Mu Darid, and to the south, the Thiri Pyit Saya palace site founded in 344 CE by King Thay Le Kyaung. The new town was planned on a grid of about 65 by 165 metres, taking into account locations of visible ancient monuments but unfortunately not the subsurface archaeology (Weise 2013, 2015b).

An opportunity to include local community in the process of nominating Bagan as a World Heritage site arose through the newly elected government. The team working on the management plan initially had great difficulty involving community representatives in discussions but this changed as soon as the democratically elected government was in place. The recently politically empowered community comprising of long-time inhabitants of the ancient villages were able to get involved in the nomination process for World Heritage status by participating in decisions on key management issues. They took the lead in discussing the future of Bagan based on issues relating to conserving heritage, improving agriculture while considering subsurface archaeology, ensuring sustainable tourism and improving their resilience to natural hazards.

During the initial phases of discussing the management of Bagan between 2013 and 2015, local community representatives were invited by the Department of Archaeology and UNESCO Consultants working on the management plan to join in talks that took place mainly in the hall of the Bagan Museum. During this time of transitional government, it was not clear how the reform movement would turn out and it was fearful for local people to stand up and express themselves in front of the authorities. Very few did, and there were also some who used the opportunity to bring up issues of previous repression and injustice. Because of this, the government authorities were initially hesitant to continue these discussions but once the initial anger had subsided, more constructive talks were initiated. This was the beginning of mainstreaming community involvement into site management.

A change in the attitude and participation of the communities took place after the elections in November 2015, and the establishment of the democratically elected government. Decentralization of the Provincial Government was initiated with the Chief Minister in Mandalay being given far-reaching powers and the people were represented by elected Members of Parliament. However, the new system was a challenge to a society that had been under military rule and repression for half a century. The capacity of the government members was also an issue as well as procedures for decision-making. The government was still uncertain how to deal with community and community members were unclear of their rights and responsibilities.

The significance of Bagan to the Buddhist communities throughout Myanmar became evident with the damage that was caused by the Chauk Earthquake on 24th August 2016. Within hours of news of the destruction spreading, voluntary groups throughout the country organized and

Fig. 10.3 Volunteers removing earthquake damage from the Sula-Mani Temple at Bagan

hired mini-trucks, generators and equipment needed to clear the damaged sites. Many drove to Bagan to help assist in emergency response (Fig. 10.3). At the same time, efforts were underway to cordon off the damaged monuments to ensure the safety of visitors, protection of the monuments, as well as to introduce logical and systematic salvaging procedures. A team from the International Centre for the Study of the Preservation and Restoration of Cultural Property (ICCROM) provided training in salvaging methodologies. The local communities however were impatient and hundreds gathered to remove the collapsed concrete spire at the Sulemani Temple and, during the process, some original elements were lost. However, it was necessary to accept the significance of the concern, motivation and drive shown by the community groups. Teams put together by celebrities also came to do hands-on work. Community cash donations totalled some $5.35 million and such involvement is illustrative of how engaged local resources can mobilise quickly to protect and maintain their living cultural heritage (Weise 2016).

At this time, the local community expressed concerns regarding the boundaries of the proposed World Heritage site, worrying that World Heritage would restrict them from improving their livelihood. With past experience in their minds, they even feared being evicted from their land as happened in 1990. But the monuments are revered by the local communities living within the heritage site, and everyone agreed that heritage must be safeguarded whilst also improving people's livelihood and standard of living. However, often the people's sentiments and concerns were not considered and the voices of individuals with vested interests took precedent (Weise 2015b: 103).

With a new National government in place, the authorities tried to ensure that communities were consulted and decisions were only taken with their consent. This was, however, innovative and neither Government nor public seemed sure of procedures. Members of Parliament who attended meetings stated their dislike of boundaries without explanation or providing alternatives. Several community interaction sessions were organized by the team preparing the management process to discuss the boundaries as well as the overall management plan. Once again community members initially stood up and lambasted the government, often targeting the Department of Archaeology. However, over time this mellowed and more constructive discussions ensued.

In my capacity as facilitator for the preparation of the management plan, whenever I visited Bagan, concerned community members would discuss with me issues concerning World Heritage proposal, including how they should respond to the Regional Government which was sceptical about the need for World Heritage status. It seemed that the Regional Government in Mandalay had little understanding of the concerns of the local communities. From the perception of the local community projects being carried out, such as road widening and viewing platforms for tourists, were not going to benefit them.

10.5   Sustainable Living Cultural Heritage Sites

Over the past decades, focus has been on safeguarding the monuments and this has been carried out in an authoritarian manner, for example with people being relocated away from Old Bagan. In the contemporary western approach to conservation, truthful expression of the original was ensured through material authenticity. Such an approach has been questioned (ICOMOS 1994). After the Chauk Earthquake of 2016 there was great pressure from the communities to restore and, where necessary, rebuild the living monuments. Such sentiments are linked to a very different understanding of the significance of heritage.

The global approach to defining and safeguarding heritage has been changing over the past decades. It is not only the exclusive monument linked to the rich and powerful in history that is considered significant, but also the continuity or traces that remain of stories depicting the lives of the common people. In Bagan, to move to a more inclusive understanding of the heritage site, archaeological research is required to find out where and how the local communities lived in the past. This study would need to be linked to understanding the existing communities living in villages that were established even before the grand monuments were built during the Bagan period between the eleventh and thirteenth centuries CE.

Such an inclusive definition of heritage encompasses numerous perceptions of any given attribute of the heritage site. This requires a system to be established that allows for dialogue and consensus building and means that management must be participatory instead of authoritarian. The approach to conservation would be to develop consent and safeguard credible expression of its significance. Living monuments go through change. The religious communities often do not accept partially damaged monuments such as monuments that do not have their spires.

It has therefore been necessary to ensure the regular restoration of these monuments. In many cases, restoration leads to further embellishments such as gilding or changing roofing from tiles to copper sheeting. Ideally, these changes must however be carried out using traditional technology within the cultural contexts to which they belong.

The Buddhist Sangha also have an important role to play in respect of ensuring the continuity of religious and cultural aspects of community life, and need to support cultural expression of local communities. The Sangha could also take an oversight function of local governance. Elected representatives of the people need to take on the role of presenting the overall concerns of their community in the consensus-building process and would then also need to go back to their community and create awareness on issues dealing with broader political, social and development concerns. Such dialogue has only just begun in Myanmar under the new democratic movement. However, the community is quickly becoming aware of their roles and responsibilities which bodes well for ensuring continuity of cultural expression.

References

Gavrilovic, P. (1992). *Repair and Strengthening of Selected Monuments in Pagan, Myanmar: Assignment Report, Conservation of Cultural Heritage at Selected Sites in Myanmar.* Unpublished UNESCO/UNDP Report.

Gavrilovic, P., Pichard, P., & Pottier, C. (2016). *Overview of Monuments Condition at Bagan: A Restoration Perspective.* Unpublished UNESCO Bangkok/Yangon Report.

ICOMOS. (1994). *The Nara Document on Authenticity.* Paris: ICOMOS.

ICOMOS. (1997). *ICOMOS Evaluation of World Heritage Nomination: Bagan No. 796.* Paris: ICOMOS.

Lunsford, R. L. (2012). *Propositions for the Conservation-Restoration of Mural Paintings and Carved Stuccoes in Bagan, Union of Myanmar: Technical & Mission Report: Assistance for the Safeguarding of the Cultural Heritage of Myanmar.* Unpublished UNESCO Bangkok Report.

MORAC/GOM. (2018). *Nomination Dossier for Inscription on the World Heritage List Bagan: Vol 1–5.* Nay Pyi Taw: Ministry of Religious Affairs and Culture, Government of Republic of the Union of Myanmar.

Nishimura, Y. (1996). *Master Plan for the Preservation of the Historic Area of Pagan: Phase I (Draft) for the Government of the Union of Myanmar.* Unpublished UNESCO Bangkok Report.

Pichard, P. (1992–2001). *Inventory of Monuments at Pagan: Volumes I–VIII.* Paris: UNESCO.

Pichard, P. (2012). *Bagan Condition of the Site and Monuments Mission Report: Capacity Building to Safeguard Cultural Heritage in Myanmar.* Unpublished UNESCO Bangkok Report.

Weise, K. (2013). *Survey Mission to Bagan Archaeological Area and Monuments, Myanmar: Institutional Capacity and Resources for the Management of Bagan.* Unpublished UNESCO Bangkok/Yangon Report.

Weise, K. (2014). *Establishing a Management System for Bagan Archaeological Area and Monument: Report on Mission to Myanmar.* Unpublished UNESCO Bangkok/Yangon Report.

Weise, K. (2015a). *Report on Inspection Carried Out on 18 August 2015 on Damage Done by Heavy Rain in Bagan and Recommendations for Emergency Assistance.* Unpublished UNESCO Bangkok/Yangon Report.

Weise, K. (2015b). *Defining Bagan Archaeological Area and Monuments Comprehensive Planning Strategy: the Integrated Management System.* Unpublished UNESCO Bangkok/Yangon Report.

Weise, K. (2016). *Chauk Earthquake 24 August 2016: Earthquake Response and Rehabilitation.* Unpublished UNESCO Bangkok/Yangon Report.

CHAPTER 11

Communities, Identities, Conflict and Appropriation in South Asia

Robin Coningham and Nick Lewer

Abstract This chapter examines challenges and controversies for heritage protection and archaeologists in two further case studies from South Asia: the impact caused by the construction of Lahore's Orange Metro Line in Pakistan and the destruction and post-disaster recording of Jaffna Fort in Sri Lanka. The examples highlight potentially contentious factors that can be brought to the surface during archaeological excavations and initiatives to protect heritage in locations of economic development and politically charged or security sensitive locations. Coningham and Lewer point to the close nexus of archaeology, heritage and identity and remind us that there are limits within which we work and that there are limits to what we can achieve in heritage protection.

Keywords Politics · Security · Identity · Heritage protection

R. Coningham (✉)
Durham University, Durham, UK
e-mail: r.a.e.coningham@durham.ac.uk

N. Lewer
Coral Associates Ltd, North Yorkshire, UK
e-mail: nick.lewer@coralassociates.org

© The Author(s) 2019
R. Coningham and N. Lewer (eds.), *Archaeology, Cultural Heritage Protection and Community Engagement in South Asia*,
https://doi.org/10.1007/978-981-13-6237-8_11

151

11.1   INTRODUCTION: BROADER INFLUENCES ON HERITAGE PROTECTION

The previous chapters have recorded and described the pressures which threaten heritage sites across South Asia. Ranging from the impacts of increasing urbanization and the rapid development of infrastructure to those arising from increasing numbers of visitors and pilgrims to places of heritage value, the case studies have also noted initiatives to protect, preserve and present a range of sites from prehistoric remains to intangible heritage.

Monuments and sites across South Asia are subject to degradation from natural processes, some sudden and others more gradual. The former is epitomized by events like the 2004 Indian Ocean Tsunami, which caused over 280,000 fatalities and $19.9 billion damage but also substantial destruction of heritage sites on the Indian and Sri Lankan coastlines (Pushparatnam 2005). Similarly, the 2016 Gorkha Earthquake killed over 9000 people, injured 22,000 and caused $10 billion damage as well as damage to 691 historic monuments, of which 131 collapsed (Coningham et al. 2018: 160). More gradual natural processes cause fewer fatalities but can be equally damaging to monuments and sites. For example, salination has destroyed brick structures within the Bronze Age cities of Harappa and Mohenjo-daro in Pakistan (Goudie 2013: 261).

South Asia's heritage has also been targeted by international and resident communities. These include the attack on the Sacred Bodhi Tree shrine in the Sri Lankan city of Anuradhapura by the Liberation Tigers of Tamil Elam (LTTE) in 1985; the demolition of the Babri Masjid in the Indian city of Ayodhya in 1992 and retaliatory damage to Hindu temples in Pakistan and Bangladesh; the bombing of the Temple of the Buddha's Tooth in Kandy, Sri Lanka, by the LTTE in 1998 (Coningham and Lewer 1999); the destruction of the Bamiyan Buddhas by the Taliban in Afghanistan in 2001; the destruction of pre-Islamic displays in the Maldives' National Museum in Male in 2012; and the bombing of the Buddhist Shrine at Bodhgaya in India in 2013 (Coningham and Young 2015: 96–99).

As these are widely published events, we will look in this chapter at two further examples from South Asia: the impact caused by the construction of Lahore's Orange Metro Line in Pakistan and the destruction and post-disaster recording of Jaffna Fort in Sri Lanka. These have broader political, economic and social ramifications for archaeologists, for communities associated with the sites, and for those who have vested interests linked to the excavations.

11.2 Lahore's Orange Metro Line

Home to one-third of the world's population and generating $1.854 trillion of its gross domestic product, South Asia has a corresponding richness of heritage with at least two separate Neolithics and two independent urbanizations, the Indus and Early Historic (Coningham and Young 2015: 3). This wealth is mirrored by Pakistan, where UNESCO World Heritage Sites include Mohenjo-daro, Takht-i-Bahi, Taxila, Thatta, Rohtas Fort and Lahore Fort and the Shalamar Gardens. The Shalamar Gardens were jointly inscribed on UNESCO's list World Heritage Sites with Lahore's Fort in 1981. Completed in 1641 CE, the 17-hectare complex contains pavilions and baths is set around formally planned tanks, paths, waterfalls and canals (Nadiem 1996: 124). The World Heritage Committee (WHC) particularly noted that its design of descending terraces represented an example of highly advanced hydraulic engineering, allowing water pressure to feed the fountains and waterfalls (Fatma 2012: 1272).

Although South Asia's cultural heritage is rich, there is increasing pressure on monuments, cityscapes and landscapes from agriculture intensification, resource extraction, urbanization, industrialization and investment in mega-infrastructure. As this volume has demonstrated, the balance between heritage and development is difficult and requires a complex multi-agency approach. Despite the fact that the Shalamar's hydraulic design was protected as an integral part of its site's UNESCO Outstanding Universal Value (OUV) and Pakistan's 1975 Antiquities Act, two of the Shalamar's three water reservoirs were destroyed when the Government of Punjab widened the old Moghul Grand Trunk Road (GT) in 1999 UNESCO's WHC consequently placed the Shalamar Gardens on UNESCO's "In Danger" list in 2000 until it was removed by a programme of mitigation in 2012.

Four years later, China Railway-Norinco observed that rapid population growth in Lahore, accompanied by rises in vehicle ownership, had intensified congestion as there was a daily transport demand of 6.8 million person trips. As a result, the Government of Punjab obtained a loan of $1.6 billion to fund the 27.1 kilometres long Orange Line. Partially meeting Lahore's transport challenges, National Engineering Services

Pakistan (NESPAK) stated that it would "greatly benefit the commuters by providing better quality and environmentally friendly public transport, reducing the number of vehicles on the road, reducing fuel consumption and consequently air emissions from vehicular exhaust especially in case of traffic congestion" (NESPAK 2016: 2). Serving 24 stations, 25.4 kilometres of its length is elevated on viaducts typically 10.97 metres high and spaced between 10 and 27 metres apart. The remaining 1.72 kilometres is underground within a cut-and-cover scheme and the Government reduced overall costs by following the course of the old GT route.

This choice brought the line within the 200 foot legal protective zones of the Shalamar Gardens, Gulabi Bagh's Gateway, Buddhu's Tomb, Chauburji and Zaib-un-Nisa's Tomb (protected by the 1975 Antiquities Act) and the Lakshmi Building, General Post Office, Lahore High Court/Aiwan-e-Auqaf Building, Saint Andrew's Church, Supreme Court Registry Building and Mauj Darya Shrine (protected by the 1985 Punjab Special Premises (Preservation) Ordinance). The dramatic impact on the monuments is illustrated here by Maryam Hussain's photograph of Chauburji (Fig. 11.1). In May 2016, the Director-General of Archaeology (Government of Punjab) issued No Objection Certificates (NOCs) to approve contraventions of the Act and the Ordinance based on a report from his Directorate, a Heritage Impact Assessment (HIA) conducted by Kolachi, Khan and Associates and a study of the control of vibrations, noise and foundations for the protection of heritage sites (Kolachi et al. 2016). Surprisingly, while the consultants identified risk of vibrations, noise and visual pollution from the piling and the construction of the 12-metre high viaduct adjacent to the World Heritage Site, they only suggested mitigations of landscaping, naming stations after the heritage site and sympathetically designing stations.

Almost unprecedented in Pakistan, however, community groups were unconvinced by the issuing of the NOCs and HIA, and cases were brought against the Government of Punjab. The community, with the support of newspaper reporters, won their initial case and the Lahore High Court stayed the construction around Shalimar and five monuments in August 2016. This forced the Director-General of Archaeology to re-issue NOCs in the correct procedure, followed by the Government of Punjab lodging a Supreme Court appeal. Despite the stay around key monuments, the Government completed the work elsewhere along the line. UNESCO's WHC voiced its concerns, noting the absence of a

Fig. 11.1 Viaduct foundation for the Orange Metro Line beside the Chauburji Gateway in Lahore

"comprehensive Heritage Impact Assessment in line with the ICOMOS Guidelines" making it "unclear on which grounds the State Party concluded that the Orange Line Metro project would have no negative impacts on the OUV of the property, nor on what basis the Department of Archaeology of the Government of Punjab issued a Non-objection Certificate" and "recommended that the (World Heritage) Committee immediately inscribe the property on the List of World Heritage in Danger" (UNESCO 2017a: 27).

In view of the potential severity of the impact on the site's OUV, UNESCO proposed the mobilization of an expert Reactive Monitoring Mission in line with its operational guidelines (UNESCO 2017b). Despite being a signatory of the 1972 Convention, the Federal Government of Pakistan did not approve the mobilization and the expert mission could not be sent. Meanwhile, construction continued until almost all of it was completed with the exception of the 200-foot protective buffer around the five monuments. UNESCO's World Heritage Secretariat drafted a resolution to place the WHS on the "In Danger" list in the summer of 2017 but the WHC, made up of signatory states, decided not to follow their advice or that of their expert advisory bodies.

Pakistan's Supreme Court set aside the High Court's stay, dismissed the civil petition and refused leave to Appeal. Having identified 31 conditions ranging from "The appellant shall make all necessary arrangements to ensure that the monuments remain stable and undamaged in all respects during the execution of the Project as specified in the HIA and Study of Control of Vibration, Noise and Foundation" to "The decorative motifs of Shalamar Garden would be replicated on the train station near the Shalamar Garden to create harmony with the Garden", the Orange Line is now being completed (Supreme Court of Pakistan 2016). Given the fact that construction recommenced, there was real concern that this World Heritage Site would be placed on the 'In Danger' list or be removed from UNESCO's List entirely. As the German city of Dresden's Cultural Landscape was deleted in 2009, following the construction of a motorway across the Elbe in 2009, such a decision was not unexpected. Despite the recommendation of the 2018 UNESCO-ICOMOS Mission to Lahore that the WHC "place the World Heritage property 'Fort and Shalamar Gardens in Lahore' on the List of World Heritage in Danger, in order to enable the State Party to show its good will for cooperation and to proceed immediately with the full and exhaustive implementation of all mitigation measures and recommendations proposed in the present report" (UNESCO 2018: 40), the WHC decided not to act. Although it failed to halt the damage to Lahore's heritage, civic action mobilized and engaged residents and educated them as to the very real threats to heritage from mega-infrastructure as well as to the potential strength of their collective voices.

11.3   Jaffna's Dutch Fort

Emerging from a 26-year civil war in 2009, Sri Lanka is now addressing associated humanitarian and cultural impacts as well as trying to establish a roadmap for national reconciliation (Lewer 2017). While efforts are addressing humanitarian challenges, damaged cultural heritage in war zones has only recently been appreciated for its potential contribution to peace-building and economic development through tourism

(Pushparatnam 2014). One such badly affected monument is Jaffna Fort, which had its ramparts partly demolished and most of the structures within its 22 hectares destroyed, including the 1706 CE Dutch Kruys Kerk church. Initially established by the Portuguese in 1618, their quadrangular fort was remodelled as a five-sided Fort by the Dutch after capturing it in 1658 CE (Nelson 1984). Despite detailed knowledge of its later history as one of the largest colonial forts in Asia, little is known of its early sequences below the colonial ruins.

Recent investment from the Dutch Government, in collaboration with the Department of Archaeology (Government of Sri Lanka) (DoA), has sponsored the conservation of Jaffna Fort's ramparts and gateway as well as structures within the interior, such as Queen's House. This work was accompanied by the excavation of deep engineering cuts, from which were recovered Early Historic Rouletted Ware as well as medieval Islamic and Chinese ceramics. The news of this discovery by the DoA and University of Jaffna was welcomed by observers, one of which stated that the "Antiquity of Jaffna city goes back to Roman times" and that "Heritage studies of a land are a prerogative of free people of that land...for the first time in decades, a Jaffna university team is allowed to participate in archaeological work" (Tamilnet 1/3/2011). These materials are well represented in Jaffna's Archaeological Museum, as well as the University of Jaffna's Archaeology Museum, and have affinities elsewhere within the island (Carswell et al. 2013; Coningham 2006). They also hint at the antiquity and depth of cultural occupation within Jaffna as well as its potential historic role within South Asia and Indian Ocean trade networks (Begley 1996; Rajan and Raman 1994).

The first season of the Jaffna Post-Disaster Archaeological Research Project was undertaken in 2017 by the University of Jaffna, Central Cultural Fund (CCF) and Durham's UNESCO Chair (Coningham et al. 2017). Excavations were conducted at Queen's House, the Old Prison and Kruys Kerk and identified earlier phases of colonial construction but also pre-colonial deposits at the Old Prison. Confirming Professor Pushparatnam's earlier reports, the excavations revealed an abundance of pre-colonial contact material, including ceramics which firmly link Jaffna to the wider Indian Ocean, such as Black and Red ware (c. 1000 BCE–100 CE), Grey Ware (c. 500 BCE–200 CE) Rouletted Ware (200 BCE–200 CE) and Red Polished Ware (c. 100 BCE–800 CE) onto contact with the west Asian world through Sasanian-Islamic Wares (c. 200

BC–800 CE) as well as evidence of trade with East Asia including discoveries of Yue Green Wares (c. 800–900 CE), Dusun Stoneware (c. 700–1100 CE) and Ming Porcelain (c. 1300–1600 CE). While we await the measurement of radiocarbon samples, preliminary analysis of the material points towards Jaffna's long history of cosmopolitanism and centrality in international trade and communication networks before and beyond European contact and has begun to aid our understanding the earlier archaeological sequences of Jaffna Fort, and northern Sri Lanka more generally (Davis et al. 2018).

Excavations at the Kruys Kerk also afforded the opportunity to co-produce a method for the removal and recording of debris from heritage structures that had been damaged by recent conflict in advance of conservation and reconstruction. Based on a methodology devised for heritage in post-earthquake Kathmandu (Nepal) (Coningham et al. 2018), pilot post-disaster clearance excavations were conducted in the north-east corner of the ruined Kruys Kerk (Fig. 11.2). The approach implemented allowed for the systematic and spatially controlled removal of rubble and also the recycling of rare materials, such as coral and Dutch bricks, that could be reused in any rehabilitation efforts. In addition to our excavation activities, Unmanned Aerial Vehicle (UAV) survey and Ground Penetrating Radar Survey (GPR) of Jaffna Fort was undertaken to identify and characterize the morphology of standing remains at the site, as well as its subsurface heritage. UAV survey confirmed the presence of three earlier semi-circular Portuguese bastions incorporated within the Dutch period fortifications and GPR survey identified the presence of several anomalies that appear to indicate walls near the site's centre within the old Dutch Parade Ground (Davis et al. 2018).

Building on the 2017 British Academy and Institute of Medieval and Early Modern Studies funding, Durham University's UNESCO Chair proposed a second season of collaborative fieldwork with the CCF and University of Jaffna with funding secured from a HEFCE Global Research Challenges Fund grant in 2018. Focusing on the quadrangle measuring 30 by 30 metres, picked up by the GPR in the middle of the Dutch Parade Ground, excavations revealed what we believe to the foundations of an earlier Portuguese church. It also revealed earlier pre-colonial phases of activity below, which have now been sampled for scientific dating. Outside the Fort, we undertook UAV survey and GPR survey of locations within Jaffna town to map and identify earlier phases of human activity outside the Fort, and we will use these to develop an

Fig. 11.2 Trainees from the Central Cultural Fund and University of Jaffna clearing brick and coral blocks from the ruins of the Kruys Kerk in Jaffna Fort

Archaeological Risk Map for Jaffna Fort and its environs to aid site managers in the protection of heritage in advance of development of urban infrastructure and tourism, which we identified as a growing trend.

These results were presented to the community through a public workshop held at the University of Jaffna and the co-design and printing of guide leaflets. Printed in English, Tamil and Sinhala, together with a trilingual temporary museum exhibition at the Fort, they meet the requests from half of surveyed visitors to the Fort ($n = 198$) for greater information and guidance (Fig. 11.3). Visitor numbers to the exhibition are currently being recorded in order to evaluate the impact of the displays on visitors and their understanding of Jaffna's deep past. A total of 132 visitors (55 foreign, 44 Tamil and 36 Sinhalese) were interviewed as part of handicraft, gift and souvenir pricing and marketability survey, which confirmed that the most popular were all locally Jaffna-made clay

Fig. 11.3 Visitors to the temporary museum exhibition in Jaffna Fort

items, particularly jewellery. It is anticipated that the Fort will provide a space for the local cooperative to sell clay items to visitors.

While many reporters welcomed the results and analysis, a number of negative commentaries were delivered by *Tamilnet*, whose criticisms appeared to focus on the fact that foreign and Sri Lankan institutions were working with the University of Jaffna and that most of the project's funding had been raised from foreign sources. Presumably their objection was that foreign and Sinhalese influenced excavation teams would produce a biased interpretation of archaeological findings. They were also critical of the proposed development of the fort as a focus for sustainable tourism to preserve Jaffna's tangible and intangible heritage as they perceived it as encouraging tourism from southern Sri Lanka which could affect local social and cultural norms. It could be countered that these perceptions do not agree with research data which shows that the Fort is currently visited by a wide spectrum of the Sri Lankan community including Sinhalese from outside of Jaffna, displaced Jaffna residents, Muslim communities returning to Jaffna, and international Tamil diaspora. Such reactions are to be expected when excavating sites that have been deeply affected by, and part of, violent internal conflicts. These might be related to human rights issues, events that happened during the conflict, disputes over the return of appropriated land, and those of missing persons.

11.4 Conclusion

The examples of the Orange Line and Jaffna Fort highlight a number of potentially contentious factors that can be brought to the surface during archaeological excavations and initiatives to protect heritage in locations of economic development, and politically charged or security sensitive locations. While civic action did mobilize, engage and educate Pakistanis to threats to heritage from mega-infrastructure projects, ultimately their concerns and those of the WHC were overruled by greater development needs linked to national economic growth and urban transport requirements. Higher political muscle and corporation lobbying were more influential, in line with the analysis of some earlier WHC decisions (Bertacchini et al. 2016). Clearly, it was decided that risks to important national heritage were worth taking so that construction targets could be met and profits achieved. There are limits to advocacy by international bodies such as the WHC and activism by people and communities engaged in heritage protection in the face of powerful vested interest.

Excavations at Jaffna Fort remind us of the sensitivity of archaeological excavations in post-war locations. Some commentators linked the perception of location "ownership" and the historical interpretation of finds to issues of identity and fears that the excavation team were (a) interested in supporting one view of history, and (b) were involved in suppressing the truth about what was being discovered. This is despite a programme of information, openness and the inclusion of Tamil, Sinhalese and foreign archaeologists. In this case, the post-war context directly impacted on the excavations; national reconciliation still has a long way to go and many in the ethnic communities still view each other with distrust and suspicion.

Clearly, we need to remember the close nexus of archaeology, heritage and identity (Coningham and Lewer 2000). In such a context, it is worth reflecting on the words of Romila Thapar: "There is also the problem of selecting items of heritage. Such choices alter the self-perception of a society. The politics that determine such selections should be evident but are often hidden...Colonial policy had a major role in selecting the heritage of modern India. Political intervention in identifying or evaluating heritage often continues under a different guise. The political use of the past is an ancient practice, but in our times we recognize it more easily" (2016: 2). These are certainly in tune with the pessimistic conclusion offered by Eric Hobsbawm: "I used to think that the profession of history, unlike that of, say, nuclear physics, could at least do no harm. Now I know it can. Our studies can turn into bomb factories like the workshops in which the IRA has learned to transform chemical fertilizer into an explosive. This state of affairs affects us in two ways. We have a responsibility to historical facts in general, and for criticizing the politico-ideological abuse of history in particular" (Hobsbawm 1992: 62–63). Both statements remind us that there are limits within which we work and that there are limits to what we can achieve.

REFERENCES

Begley, V. (1996). *Ancient Port of Arikamedu: New Excavations and Researches 1989–1992*. Paris: Ecole Francais D'Extreme-Orient.

Bertacchini, E., Liuzza, C., Meskell, L., & Saccone, D. (2016). The Politicization of UNESCO World Heritage Decision Making. *Public Choice, 167*(1–2), 95–129.

Carswell, J. S., Deraniyagala, S. U., & Graham, A. (2013). *Mantai: City by the Sea*. Aichwald: Linden Soft.

Coningham, R. A. E. (2006). *Anuradhapura: The British-Sri Lankan Excavations at Anuradhapura Salgaha Watta 2, Volume 2: The Artefacts*. Oxford: Archaeopress.

Coningham, R. A. E., Acharya, K. P., Davis, C. E., Weise, K., Kunwar, R. B., & Simpson, I. A. (2018). Look Down, Not Up: Protecting the Post-disaster Subsurface Heritage of the Kathmandu Valley's UNESCO World Heritage Site. In L. A. Bracken, H. Ruszczyk, & T. Robinson (Eds.), *Evolving Narratives of Hazard and Risk: The Gorkha Earthquake, Nepal, 2015* (pp. 159–181). London: Palgrave Macmillan.

Coningham, R. A. E., & Lewer, N. (1999). Paradise Lost: The Bombing of the Temple of the Tooth—a UNESCO World Heritage Site in Sri Lanka. *Antiquity, 73*, 857–866.

Coningham, R. A. E., & Lewer, N. (2000). Identity and Archaeology in South Asia: Interpretations and Consequences. *Antiquity, 74*, 664–667.

Coningham, R. A. E., Manuel, M. J., Davis, C. E., & Gunawardhana, P. (2017). Archaeology and Cosmopolitanism in Early Historic and Medieval Sri Lanka. In Z. Biedermann & A. Strathern (Eds.), *Sri Lanka at the Crossroads of History* (pp. 19–43). London: UCL Press.

Coningham, R. A. E., & Young, R. L. (2015). *The Archaeology of South Asia: From the Indus to Asoka*. Cambridge: Cambridge University Press.

Davis, C. E., Gunawadhana, P., Coningham, R. A. E., Pushparatnam, P., Schmidt, A., Manuel, M. J., et al. (2018). Recent Excavations and Survey at Jaffna Fort in 2017 and Reflections on the Antiquity of Indian Ocean Trade. In P. Gunawardhana & R. A. E. Coningham (Eds.), *Buddha Rashmi Vesak Volume 2018* (pp. 67–78). Colombo: Central Cultural Fund of Sri Lanka.

Fatma, S. (2012). Waterworks in Mughal Gardens. *Proceedings of the Indian History Congress, 73*, 1268–1278.

Goudie, A. (2013). *Arid and Semi-arid Geomorphology*. Cambridge: Cambridge University Press.

Hobsbawm, E. (1992, December 16). The New Threat to History. *New York Review of Books*, pp. 62–65.

Kolachi, B., Khan, R., & Rogers, A. P. (2016). *Heritage Impact Assessment of Lahore Orange Line Metro Train Project for Lahore Development Authority*. Unpublished Report.

Lewer, N. (2017). Tensions Between Short Term Outcomes and Long Term Peacebuilding in Post-War Sri Lanka. In M. Anstey & V. Rosoux (Eds.), *Negotiating Reconciliation in Peacemaking: Quandries of Relationship Building* (pp. 277–303). New York: Springer.

Nadiem, I. H. (1996). *Lahore: A Glorious Heritage*. Lahore: Sang-e-Meel.

National Engineering Services Pakistan (NESPAK). (2016). *Presentation to the DG of Archaeology, Government of Punjab, Pakistan*.

Nelson, W. A. (1984). *The Dutch Forts of Sri Lanka: The Military Monuments of Ceylon.* Edinburgh: Canongate.

Pushparatnam, P. (2005). *Preliminary Survey of Tsunami-Affected Monuments and Sites in the Maritime Region of Sri Lanka, Part 8: The Northern Maritime Region from Tiriyaya to Jaffna.* Colombo: ICOMOS.

Pushparatnam, P. (2014). *Tourism and Monuments: Of Archaeological Heritage in Northern Sri Lanka.* Jaffna: P. Pushparatnam.

Rajan, K. V., & Raman, K. (1994). *Kaveripattinam Excavations 1963–73: A Port City on the Tamilnadu Coast.* New Delhi: Archaeological Survey of India.

Supreme Court of Pakistan. (2016). Against Judgment Dated 19.8.2016 of Lahore High Court, Lahore, Passed in Writ Petition No. 39291 of 2015. http://www.supremecourt.gov.pk/web/user_files/File/C.M.A._8215_2016.pdf.

Tamilnet. (2011, March 1). *Antiquity of Jaffna City Goes Back to Roman Times.* https://www.tamilnet.com/art.html?catid=79&artid=33611.

Thapar, R. (2016, September 5, Monday). *Past Cultures as the Heritage of the Present.* Keynote Lecture Delivered at SOAS South Asia Institute/Presidency University Conference on 'Heritage and History in South Asia', Celebrating the Centenary of SOAS University of London. https://www.soas.ac.uk/south-asia-institute/events/heritage-and-history-in-south-asia/file116739.pdf.

UNESCO. (2017a). *State of Conservation of Properties Inscribed on the World Heritage List.* WHC/17/41.COM/7B.Add. https://whc.unesco.org/archive/2017/whc17-41com-7BAdd2-en.pdf.

UNESCO. (2017b, July 12). *Operational Guidelines for the Implementation of the World Heritage Convention.* https://whc.unesco.org/en/guidelines/.

UNESCO. (2018, June 24–July 4). *World Heritage Committee.* 42nd Session Manama, Bahrain. Item 7B of the Provisional Agenda. http://whc.unesco.org/archive/2018/whc18-42com-7BAdd2-en.pdf.

CHAPTER 12

Conclusion

Robin Coningham and Nick Lewer

Abstract This chapter summarizes aspects of location, community engagement activities and challenges that the book's case studies highlighted, and from this identifies generic and context specific threads of the role and engagement of local communities and agencies in tangible and intangible heritage protection and conservation. It then reviews methodologies and frameworks for aligning community engagement, archaeology and heritage protection and offers a practical framework (ProtectNet) that can guide a systematic process to align archaeological research methodology for the identification, protection and conservation of sites with community consultation and engagement activities, monitoring and impact assessment of engagement activities. In the final section, concerns from community and archaeological perspectives are discussed.

Keywords Heritage protection frameworks · Good practice

R. Coningham (✉)
Durham University, Durham, UK
e-mail: r.a.e.coningham@durham.ac.uk

N. Lewer
Coral Associates Ltd, North Yorkshire, UK
e-mail: nick.lewer@coralassociates.org

© The Author(s) 2019
R. Coningham and N. Lewer (eds.), *Archaeology, Cultural Heritage Protection and Community Engagement in South Asia*,
https://doi.org/10.1007/978-981-13-6237-8_12

165

12.1   INTRODUCTION

As noted in Chapter 1, this volume set out to present a series of case studies of South Asian heritage management interventions and strategies, which have sought to stimulate, develop and enhance community engagement and participation. We have incorporated a breadth of contemporary initiatives to preserve, protect and promote cultural heritage in order to contextualize and evaluate the success of the approaches and strategies adopted. We have also recognized the shared challenges facing archaeologists, heritage practitioners, policy makers and communities within the region. These include sustainability, linkages with existing community programmes and institutions, building administrative and social networks, community motivation and managing expectations of communities, the balance between local economic development (tourism) and benefit for residents, sustainability and impact assessment.

While presenting rarely reported strategies, our case studies are drawn from contributors with longitudinal experience of heritage-focused community engagement and all demonstrate the current pressures which daily threaten heritage sites. We have also drawn from extant scholarship focused on archaeology, community engagement and heritage protection from both tangible and intangible perspectives. Sourcing case studies representing Buddhist, Hindu, Islamic and other traditions from South Asian heritage management interventions and strategies, we have described and analysed the practice of community engagement by presenting contemporary initiatives that contribute to preserving, protecting and promoting cultural and natural heritage. We also acknowledge the generosity of Durham University and Durham's UNESCO Chair in allowing this chapter to be made Open Access to reach and influence as wide an audience as possible.

12.2   THREADS

This book's experienced contributors represent academics, practitioners, managers and policymakers from universities, NGOs and IGOs who met for the first time in Kathmandu at the *Heritage at Risk 2017: Pathways to the Protection and Rehabilitation of Cultural Heritage in South Asia* in September 2017. The symposium was sponsored by the UK's Arts and Humanities Research Council's Global Challenges Research Fund (AHRC-GCRF-AH/P005993/1), with support from UNESCO

Fig. 12.1 Delegates at the AHRC-GCRF 'Heritage at Risk 2017: Pathways to the Protection and Rehabilitation of Cultural Heritage in South Asia' Workshop in Kathmandu

Kathmandu, ICOMOS (Nepal) and the Department of Archaeology (Government of Nepal) (DoA) (Fig. 12.1). Collectively, their reflections present micro and macro-heritage sites at new and known locations in post-disaster and post-conflict environments, as well as those threatened by environmental and developmental challenges. The diverse, but complementary, nature of our coverage is summarized in Table 12.1.

A recurrent theme across all case studies has been the importance of the role and engagement of local communities and agencies in heritage protection. As well as the challenges noted in Chapter 1, a number of cross-cutting context specific and generic threads became apparent when compiling the presented case studies:

Generic

- The connection or disconnection of people to sites;
- The importance of local understanding and interpretation of culture and history;

Table 12.1   Geographical and thematic coverage of our 11 case studies

Case study	Location type	Community engagement activities	Challenges
Bangladesh Bhitargarh	Macro-heritage site; Developmental; Existing site	Bhitargarh festival; Traditional games; Indigenous performances; Seminars, workshops, discussion forums; Training in excavation techniques; Survey of living traditions	Imagined national political community; Private land ownership; Disconnect of migrants with the local heritage
India Bindu Sarovar Museum, Sidhpur	Macro-heritage site; New site	Seminars, workshops, discussion forums; Survey of living practices; Building a museum	Disconnect of visitors with the local heritage
Sri Lanka Kuragala	Micro-heritage site; Developmental; Post-conflict; Existing site	Limited at present; Political engagement to remove illegal structures	Religious and ethnic tensions; Encroachment and illegal construction on the site; Contested historical evidence; Politics
Nepal Dohani	Micro-heritage site; Post-conflict; Post-disaster; New site	Community consultation; Archaeological briefings; Schools activities; Archaeology club; Facebook page; Site protection committee formed; Festival	Motivation; Sustainability
Nepal Upper Mustang	Micro-heritage site; Post-conflict; Post-disaster; Existing site	Documenting and storing artefacts; Training guides; Information leaflets; Free dispensary; Training and capacity building activities; Workshops and design of micro-projects; Training in recording of inventory	Remoteness; Hostility to central authorities; Building trust; Movement of engaged local activists and artisans away from Mustang; Dispute over funding allocation

(continued)

Table 12.1 (continued)

Case study	Location type	Community engagement activities	Challenges
Pakistan Gojal Valley in Gilgit-Baltistan	Macro-heritage site; Post disaster; Existing site	Participatory mapping of resilience and intangible heritage; Conversations; Listening to stories; Participating in everyday activities; Building a museum	Articulation by community of everyday cultural practice; Poorly planned disaster resettlement houses; Resettlement of displaced persons challenges traditional pattern language and their meanings; World Food Programme aid
Nepal Community Forests	Macro-heritage site; Environmental; Post conflict; Post-disaster; Existing site	Community engagement legislation—community forests and buffer zones; Anti-poaching; Revenue generation including ecotourism	Remote communities; Ensuring pro-poor, pro-women and marginalised groups strategies in development plans; Human-wildlife conflict; Long-term support and assistance
Myanmar Bagan	Macro-heritage site; Post-disaster; Existing site	Community led reconstruction; Public consultation meetings	Political governance; Fear of authority; Communities critical and sceptical of government; Encroachment; Inappropriate reconstruction; Looting
Sri Lanka Jaffna Fort	Micro-heritage site; Post-conflict; New site	Workshops; Information leaflets; Temporary museum exhibition	Legacy of war; Inter-ethnic post conflict sensitivities including those of missing persons, human rights and reconciliation processes; Mistrust between ethnic communities; Politics
Pakistan Orange Metro Line	Macro-heritage site; Developmental; New site	Community activism through the legal system; Raising awareness of threats to heritage	Balance between heritage protection and economic development; Politics

- The links between tangible and intangible culture;
- Community engagement is important for the preservation and protection of heritage sites;
- There are limits to successful community engagement or activism because of more powerful and influential actors;
- The difficulty of commissioning longitudinal studies to measure the impact of heritage protection initiatives and economic development associated with tourism and wider infrastructure changes;
- Heritage is a knowledge resource of value to people.

Context Specific

- The influence of context on excavations and heritage protection, including post-disaster, post-conflict, environment and development;
- Whether there is contested ownership of an archaeological site;
- In some circumstances, it is dangerous for people to become engaged, for example, due to religious extremism or challenging vested interest.

12.3   METHODOLOGIES AND FRAMEWORKS FOR ALIGNING ARCHAEOLOGY, HERITAGE PROTECTION AND COMMUNITY ENGAGEMENT

12.3.1   Community Management of Protected Areas Conservation (COMPACT)

As many contributors have noted, the global investigation of the nexus of community engagement, archaeology and heritage protection is not novel and has already been explored through, for example, the COMPACT initiative of the United Nations Development Programme (UNDP) and the United Nations Foundation (UNF). As UNESCO's World Heritage Centre is one of COMPACT's founding partners, we will briefly examine this approach before we present our own methodology, as co-designed and piloted by Durham's UNESCO Chair.

COMPACT has number of principles that are echoed throughout our case studies, some of which we identified in Chapter 1. Brown and Hay-Edie give these as the importance of local community ownership, management and responsibility; the crucial role of social capital through investment in local institutions and individuals to build the capacity of communities for stewardship; sharing power, transparent processes and broad public participation along with trust, flexibility and patience; the cost-effectiveness of small grants; making a commitment over time (2014: 21). COMPACT's methodology has three parts which underpin its framework for planning and implementation (ibid. 2014: 24):

- Baseline assessment - providing a 'snapshot' of the site to analyse emerging trends and serving as a basis for future monitoring and evaluation;
- Conceptual model - a diagrammatic tool documenting site-level processes, threats and opportunities believed to impact biodiversity conservation in the area;
- Site strategy - providing an important framework for the allocation of resources; implementation of grants and other activities; and assessment of results.

Experience from COMPACT has been used to involve communities in the nomination of World Heritage Sites, including consideration of Tentative Lists and preparation of nominations. According to Brown and Hay Edie:

> Ideally, broad upstream participation will ensure that issues relating to indigenous peoples and local communities are considered at the outset of a nomination and not after the fact of designation. Involvement at this stage can help to bridge the potential separation between Outstanding Universal Value and those values held by local people. (ibid. 2014: 34)

12.3.2 Durham's UNESCO Chair Cascade Methodology and ProtectNet Framework

Excavation > Engagement

Early phases of Durham UNESCO Chair's field missions were largely focused on protecting heritage during the delivery of pilgrimage infrastructure at living sites, including Lumbini, Kathmandu and Tilaurakot-Kapilavastu in Nepal; Polonnaruva and Anuradhapura in Sri Lanka; Bagerhat, Paharpur and Mahasthangarh in Bangladesh; and Champaner-Pavagadh in India. This allowed us, and our partners, to co-produce and pilot a cascade methodology to assess, identify and map risks to subsurface archaeology within a living World Heritage context. Our cascade flows from Unmanned Aerial Vehicle (UAV) mapping and photogrammetry to field-walking, geophysical survey, auger transects, and research-oriented excavation with geoarchaeological and chronometric sampling in advance of enhanced interpretation, conservation and presentation. The resultant information forms an integral element of site management systems, with the creation of zoned Archaeological Risk Maps for each site in advance of the development of tourist, pilgrim and residential infrastructure. Initially, our cascade included the following stages:

12.3.2.1 New Sites

Phase A1: Site Investigation (Desktop research, satellite images, site visit, GPS and photographic record)

After a desktop review of reports, UAV take aerial photographs to build topographic maps for the digitization of the location of infrastructure, boundaries and monuments.

12.3.2.2 New Sites and Known Sites

Phase A2: Non-intrusive Site Assessment (Mapping, geophysical survey and field-walking)

During initial cascade developments, we offered advance briefings to stakeholders, residents and landowners. Digitized field and land use zones around sites are given individual codes and walked by archaeologists collecting surface cultural material. Spreads of surface artefacts are utilized as proxies for the presence of buried material. If field-walking identifies areas of significance then geophysics is used to map subsurface heritage.

Phase A3: Intrusive Site Assessment (Augering and excavation, and briefing meeting before the start of the field season and debriefing at the end)

Augers can recover ten-metre deep soil cores showing colour, consistency and content. This allows an understanding of underlying deposits and presence/absence of cultural material. Cores can be used to create transects across areas as well as in areas difficult to survey, such wooded areas, or where alluvial overburden may conceal cultural material below. This phase is completed with a community debriefing on results and display of artefacts. During some interactions, local communities might request additional activities, for example at Tilaurakot in Nepal, local residents asked for the conservation of excavated monuments rather than their reburial following recording.

Phase A4: Post-Excavation Work and Conservation (Publications, preparation of an Archaeological Risk Map and/or conservation work, presentation and interpretation and tourism development)

Field activities are followed by publications and interim reports, the latter with Archaeological Risk Maps and recommended management guidelines. These maps translate research and investigation into a coherent, spatial visualization of areas which contain valuable and vulnerable archaeological and heritage assets. They are a guide for designing and planning future developments, land purchase and land controls. They are not a complete map of the presence/absence of archaeological material but as an indication of risk to subsurface material. Developments within the vicinity, whether by site managers, national authorities, local government or private enterprise, should be avoided wherever possible and monitored if deemed essential.

Areas highlighted 'Very High', 'High' and even 'Medium' Risk should have no intrusive development whatsoever, everything should be 100% non-intrusive and fully reversible. 'Intrusive' activities include the use of mechanical diggers or JCBs, soil extraction, sand/silt processing, the digging of foundations and use of heavy agricultural machinery. Areas of 'Low' and 'Very Low' Risk indicate areas where there is little risk to archaeological structures or material, however, development should still be avoided where possible and should be non-intrusive and fully reversible. The five levels of risk are given traffic lights on maps for ease of use (Fig. 12.2).

The Management Guidelines accompanying the Archaeological Risk Maps are also critical and the ones for the World Heritage Site of Lumbini in Nepal were co-produced by policy makers, heritage managers, planners, conservators, archaeologists, local stakeholders and religious practitioners (Weise 2013: 182–189). Its approach was holistic with eight sections of guidelines to:

- protect the World Heritage Property and its Outstanding Universal Value;
- address the Kenzo Tange Master Plan;
- ensure an appropriate and sustainable environment;
- conserve the archaeological vestiges;

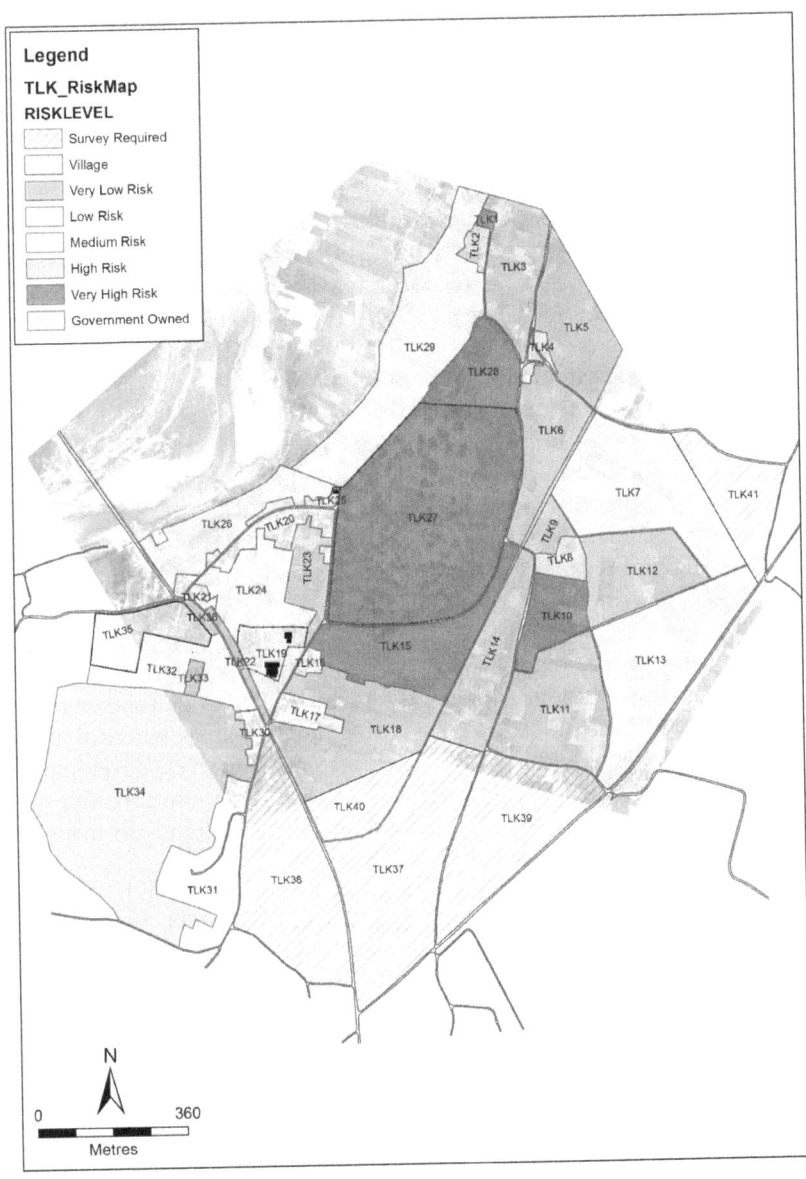

Fig. 12.2   Archaeology Risk Map prepared for the site of Tilaurakot-Kapilavastu

- provide facilities and services for visitors/pilgrims;
- regulate activities within the Sacred Garden;
- control inappropriate development;
- promote continued research and discourse.

Significantly, Guideline 48 called for the establishment of consultation processes '*to ensure the cooperation and collaboration of all stakeholders in partaking in an appropriate development of the region to ensure the safe-guarding of the cultural, natural and spiritual heritage in and around Lumbini*' (ibid.: 189).

12.3.3   Engagement > Excavation > Exhibition > Engagement

Since developing our initial cascade, and drawing from experiences of working in Nepal's Terai and elsewhere at living sites in South Asia, we now recommend embedding community engagement from the start of archaeological interventions. Indeed, as part of the wider multidiscipli-nary Japanese-Funds-in-Trust-for-UNESCO project, we have under-taken a project with the DoA and Lumbini Development Trust (LDT) to pilot the development of an extensive community consultation meth-odology to involve local communities more in archaeological investiga-tion and the future development of tourism and pilgrimage at historical sites in Kapilbastu and Rupandehi Districts in Nepal. From this study, we have prepared a framework to develop an integrated research pro-cess that enables us to systematically co-ordinate and align community consultation with the progressive stages of archaeological investigation through early site assessment, planning, conservation and implementa-tion phases.

The first stage of community consultation is a short scoping survey to gather information on local communities, including demographic data, map surrounding settlements, local knowledge and/or intangible tradi-tions associated with the site, baseline identification of activities on, at or near the site and preliminary inventories/activities that may be damaging the archaeological remains and other values related to the site, but also other uses of the site enhancing these values. This information, along with the results of archaeological investigations, will inform site man-agers on additional actions to be taken, potential liaisons to strengthen community engagement in the next stages and early considerations for local expectations and/or concerns. Data from scoping surveys also prepares for a wider community consultation in the case of archaeological investigations pursuing into the next stage of research at the site, for example, intrusive assessments.

Wider community consultation aims to explore ways in which people can be more involved in the protection of archaeological sites as well as the potential development of sites for tourism and pilgrimage. It comprises survey of a representative sample of the local communities focusing on the same general elements listed above but also additional or more specific questions that have emerged during scoping work. At the end of the consultation, a debriefing is organized with feedback from local communities on the survey results. It is also advised that additional information regarding the results of archaeological investigations be shared with local communities and liaison set up for potential collaborative actions and/or community engagement projects.

Based on the consultation, handbooks and guidelines are drafted to determine the next steps of engagement, including the type of actions or programmes that could be developed within the community, their objectives and the groups, organizations, individuals involved. An informal agreement or letter of intent can be signed by representatives of different groups and organizations involved, defining the nature of their collaboration and separating roles and tasks in the implementation of actions and programmes. Ultimately, the outcomes of the guidelines and handbooks are monitored and re-evaluated whenever required. Community consultation was coordinated by Durham's UNESCO Chair and involved staff from key national and local organizations responsible for heritage site management but also local school teachers and college lecturers and staff from local municipality, village committee, development and administrative offices. Such a survey will comprise a series of informal local workshops, community interviews and background demographic data collection.

This enhanced cascade ensures that local stakeholders, government organizations and archaeologists engage in community briefings prior to archaeological activities to identify the parameters and impacts of those investigations. To deepen understanding and cooperation between archaeologists and the community, consultations prior to the start of excavations are used and Table 12.2 provides an example of the form used at Dohani, as described in Chapter 5.

Information from such surveys contributes to archaeologists understanding community needs, local living heritage and culture more clearly

Table 12.2 Community consultation form deployed at Dohani in 2018 (Interviewer guiding questions in italics)

Date		Location	Interview number	Interviewer name

Explained project content:
Explained ethics of interview:
Obtained consent:

About interviewee

History and importance
What can you tell us about this place?
History of Samai Mai shrine:
Do you know anyone who has benefited from the shrine?
Who funded the construction of the platform and elephants?
Is the family still here? Ando do they continue to take care of it?
Why elephants? How widespread is this type of elephant shrine?
Do you know of any other archaeological sites in Dohani?

Present use of the site
What happens in the fields and land close to the site?
How do residents use the site?
Do you ever go to the site? How often? For what reason?
Expectations of local people for the site?
Does anybody look after the site?
Would you be interested in looking after the site?

Threats to the site
Do you think that any of the following things could
be a danger to the site:
• *soil excavation close to boundaries;*
• *encroachment onto the site;*
• *ownership of land near the site?*
• *economic and trading factors related to development;*
Any other threats?

Livelihoods
What are the main livelihoods in the village?
Are you using local material to earn money?
Do you have any skill to produce handicrafts?
What kind of crafts/products?
Are they sold anywhere else?
Could their production be increased?

Tourists/visitors
Do you see many tourists/pilgrims coming to visit the site?
If so, do you know where they are from? And why do they visit?
Would you like to see more people visiting the site?
Do you have any business or contact with Buddhist pilgrims?

Land
Do you own land? If so, how much land?
Where is it located? How do you use it?

Other Notes
e.g.: local organisations and groups

Table 12.3 *ProtectNet* pilot framework synchronizing archaeological investigations with community engagement

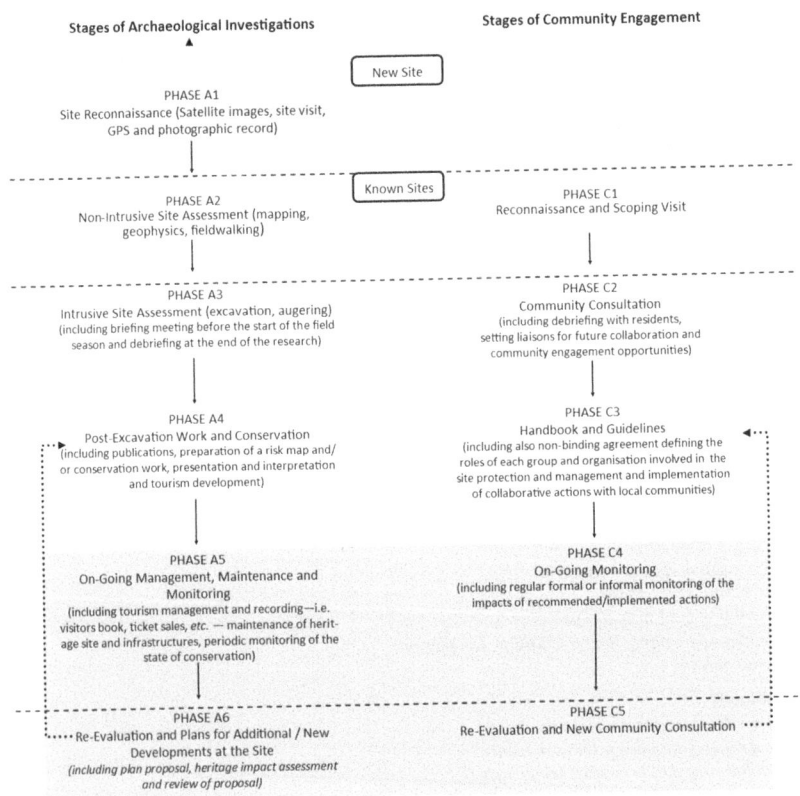

Protectnet: Micro-heritage protection through community engagement

Stages of Archaeological Investigations

Stages of Community Engagement

New Site

PHASE A1
Site Reconnaissance (Satellite images, site visit, GPS and photographic record)

Known Sites

PHASE A2
Non-Intrusive Site Assessment (mapping, geophysics, fieldwalking)

PHASE C1
Reconnaissance and Scoping Visit

PHASE A3
Intrusive Site Assessment (excavation, augering) (including briefing meeting before the start of the field season and debriefing at the end of the research)

PHASE C2
Community Consultation
(including debriefing with residents, setting liaisons for future collaboration and community engagement opportunities)

PHASE A4
Post-Excavation Work and Conservation (including publications, preparation of a risk map and/ or conservation work, presentation and interpretation and tourism development)

PHASE C3
Handbook and Guidelines
(including also non-binding agreement defining the roles of each group and organisation involved in the site protection and management and implementation of collaborative actions with local communities)

PHASE A5
On-Going Management, Maintenance and Monitoring
(including tourism management and recording—i.e. visitors book, ticket sales, *etc.* — maintenance of heritage site and infrastructures, periodic monitoring of the state of conservation)

PHASE C4
On-Going Monitoring
(including regular formal or informal monitoring of the impacts of recommended/implemented actions)

PHASE A6
Re-Evaluation and Plans for Additional / New Developments at the Site
(including plan proposal, heritage impact assessment and review of proposal)

PHASE C5
Re-Evaluation and New Community Consultation

and can therefore contemplate pragmatic engagement strategies. Such a process allows a more meaningful engagement in a systematic and planned manner that promotes the involvement of local people in the design of heritage protection measures, tourism approaches, and potential generation of income associated with sites. Drawing from COMPACT, Durham's Cascade and community consultation methodologies have formulated a guiding framework called *ProtectNet* to synchronize archaeological investigation with community engagement (Table 12.3).

12.4   GOOD PRACTICE: SOME CONCLUDING REFLECTIONS

12.4.1   Resistance

This book has supported and argued for the proposition that archaeologists engaged in ethical practice in South Asia should see community engagement as an important and fully integrated part of their activities. This includes interacting and articulating with colleagues working in tourism, relief, community development and environmental sectors, and making links with NGOs, GOs, IGOs, universities and research organizations to help understand further conceptual and theoretical underpinnings of community engagement. Our case studies have identified engagement methodologies and approaches that point to, and illustrate, good practice. This is, of course, a big ask of technical teams who are often working to their limit in terms of human and financial resources and it is important to note that resistance to this approach may be encountered:

> We can't keep going back to the community to clear everything with them. There are too many opinions and interests. We just wouldn't be able to get our work done. Most people are ignorant, and they don't know anything about what should be done or what we are doing. Why ask them? (Interview, Kathmandu, 2018)

A concern raised by archaeologists relates to the extent that they become involved with a community, and how the boundaries of their engagement can be clearly defined. For example, is an objective of archaeological-based community engagement also to impact on the social fabric and social capital more widely? Could it help build civic pride, or help reduce prejudice between contesting identity groups for example? Should such objectives be specifically built into community engagement programmes or is this too much to expect? Discussions need to be developed before an intervention so that objectives and expectations are clear for both the archaeology team and the community.

From the community perspective, the key observation is the need for systematic, coordinated and sustained engagement with local people by government agencies, donors, reconstruction and archaeological teams and associated stakeholders. People living close to archaeological and reconstruction sites often have a deep spiritual connection with temples and other heritage monuments that have been built up over long periods. There is a danger that this aspect will be lost if this connection is not respected by restorers and those tasked with reconstruction or conservation. One interviewee told us at the earthquake damaged Jaisidewal Temple in Kathmandu:

> We don't feel part of all this work and nobody tells us anything or asks our advice, and I now have less interest in looking after the place. It doesn't seem like ours. So, I'm not going to stop people or tell them off for using it to dry their clothes or sell things from it. Just an information board would be a start. Some people did talk with us but nothing happened. (Interview, Kathmandu, 2018)

As a result, people become rather cynical when they are interviewed or questioned again under the guise of engagement, and therefore have little enthusiasm to become involved with projects that, despite the rhetoric of inclusion and participation, are still defined by outsiders and dependent on their money. People can see that they are not usually involved in any 'high level' decision-making that affects them, that their voice is not directly heard at the academic, policy and research conferences and meetings where plans are instigated, and that they are being consulted as part of a 'box ticking' exercise at the end of a long line of other more 'important' or powerful stakeholders.

To help overcome this attitude, we have argued for the deployment multidisciplinary teams that include community mobilizers and development specialists who can interface between communities, archaeologists and other reconstruction experts. Education and preparation is needed for both the community and the archaeologists so that communities are at the heart of reconstruction and heritage protection rather than remaining at the periphery.

12.4.2   Community Good Practice

Despite the feelings expressed by some community interviewees in the preceding section, there are many examples of people stepping-up and engaging in their heritage protection in collaboration with archaeologists and others. This may, for example, be simply agreeing to common sense guidelines such as those given in Table 12.4. These are easy to understand and cost little to disseminate.

Table 12.4 Common sense community guidelines for heritage protection

Do's	Don't's
• Visit the archaeological sites of your region; • Share your knowledge of these ancient sites; • Continue existing cultural or religious traditions at your local sites, without damaging monuments or material below the ground; • Promote respectful behaviour at archaeological sites (cleaning campaigns, no open defecation zones, welcome visitors coming to your local site, etc.)	• Do not voluntarily damage ancient monuments and archaeological sites; • Do not remove any ancient objects or materials found in an archaeological site; • Do not drive vehicles on protected archaeological sites; • Do not use excavators or machines inside or near archaeological sites; • Do not throw garbage on an archaeological site

12.5   PROSPECT

Our case studies have highlighted many examples of interventions in the name of heritage protection, some leading to the dislocation of communities from their tangible and intangible heritage, whether in the form of moving residents from Old Bagan, restricting development at Champaner-Pavagadh or the implementation of Lumbini Master Plan in the 1970s, which witnessed the relocation of seven villages. While some families were relocated nearby, commentators have noted that:

> the process of 'relocation' was conducted in a heavy-handed and 'top-down' manner. People reported that they were first asked to leave and given false promises regarding future provision of jobs and services (such as water and electricity) in new locations. Subsequently, however, they report that they were threatened and forced out from their lands and natal homes. Informants described how electricity supplies were cut, after which families were physically removed and their homes demolished before them. (Molesworth and Müller-Böker 2005: 194)

Other case studies have presented the destruction of heritage sites and their environments; both criminally targeted, as in the case of the Babri Mosque, the Bamiyan Buddhas and Kandy's Temple of the Tooth, or with judicial permission, as in the case of Nagarjunakonda, Devnimori and the mosques and temples impacted by Lahore's Orange Line. In the case of the latter intervention, while the legal rights of the tangible entity have been considered, the community's intangible rights have been afforded less consideration and protection.

We must also recognize that whenever confronted by what Nehru referred to as the "conflict between the claims of today in the sense of practical utility and the claims of the past", community consultation and engagement with local stakeholders pre and post-disaster or conflict, and in situations of accelerated development, makes good sense to help understand and document traditional models of cyclical renewal, construction methods, maintenance and ownership, and factors in the collapse or survival of monuments as well as informal non-state resilience pathways which structure lives after a disaster or dislocation. Certainly, given the urgency to rehouse people, restore public services and repair, for example, places of worship, after a disaster or conflict there is a temptation to quickly as possible to 'Build Back Better' using modern materials and construction methods. As frequently encountered by our recent British Academy Global Challenges Research Fund Cities and Infrastructure project in Kathmandu (CI170241), this can cause irreversible damage to monuments and damage valuable cultural heritage. Emergency teams and communities need practical and pragmatic training in risk reduction strategies for monuments in post-conflict and natural disaster situations keeping and preserving debris post-disaster so that it can be utilized in reconstruction programmes (Coningham et al. 2018).

This links to further ethical and political concerns of epistemic questions of how the significance of sites and destroyed heritage are determined and by whom, and how this influences their treatment in a post-disaster scenario, particularly with reference to practical and theoretical ideals for community-based research, mediation, inclusivity and ideals of joint stewardship and mutual accountability. This is pertinent because heritage can play a unifying role in post-conflict responses while unethical promotion alienates communities and can generate the destruction of that same heritage. Such concerns are valid, as short-term environmental shocks have led to a rise in intercommunal tensions, violence and political negotiation.

Looking forward, we recognize how our initial cascade from excavation to engagement represented a shift from the tradition of arbitrarily fencing the tangible noted in Chapter 3, although we are still far from the community stewardship scenarios discussed in Chapter 9. Our revised cascade strongly advocates the flow from engagement to excavation to exhibition and engagement with deliberate provision of evaluation and feedback loops. For example, we have started to pilot exhibition and education activities following exemplars presented in Chapter 2 with a Heritage Festival at Tilaurakot-Kapilavastu, generously sponsored by Dr. Tokushin Kasai. Co-designed with the DoA, LDT, local teachers and Municipality Education Officer, we launched the inaugural Tilaurakot-Kapilvastu Heritage Festival in February 2018. The one-day festival included a public excavation debriefing and tour, an exhibition of excavated artefacts and a photographic exhibition to highlight threats to local heritage sites. The exhibition also promoted local intangible heritage by showcasing the handicrafts of the Hariyali Hastakala Women's Group as well as dance displays from the Jalashaya Homestay Group, both of which belong to the indigenous Tharu community. It was also attended by over 100 pupils from 21 local schools, who participated in drawing and speech competitions. The students' artistic creations were displayed on the historic site and will soon be displayed in the refurbished local museum. Of the 60 visitors who completed a feedback sheet at the photographic exhibition, 97% stated that they were more aware of heritage protection issues after visiting.

We have also drawn on the site-specific and broader landscape based research results and experiences of Lumbini and Kathmandu and translated these into exhibitions and popular print formats. A temporary post-disaster exhibition in Kathmandu in September 2017 attracted 8079 visitors in four days. We translated this to Durham's Oriental Museum in an exhibition called 'Resilience in the Rubble', attracting 12,850 visitors between September 2017 and January 2018. Through these exhibitions, we changed public perception of the need for archaeological intervention in post-disaster scenarios as only 49% in Kathmandu and 26% in Durham had been previously aware of the value and vulnerability of subsurface remains, with attendees noting 'The narrative of reinforcement after earthquake that really shows the scale of the problems, but offers solutions for this and future disasters in terms of rescue and reconstruction' and 'I Liked the info on how training was provided for first responders, safeguarding artifacts from future earthquakes' as well as recognizing that the underpinning research 'indicated ancient people knew how to build to withstand earthquakes'. The DoA and ICOMOS (Nepal), with additional funding from the Arts and Humanities Research Council's Global Challenges Research Fund grant (AH/P006256/1), the British Academy's Global Challenges Research Fund Cities and Infrastructure Programme (CI170241) and Durham's

Institute of Medieval and Early Modern Studies (IMEMS), were central in its redesign and relocation to Kathmandu's new Earthquake Museum, which opened on the third anniversary of the 2015 Gorkha Earthquake in April 2018 with the intention of enhancing community awareness of the vulnerability of heritage in post-disaster environments.

Finally, demonstrating that 'community' can include local residents and stakeholders directly affected as well as non-resident stakeholders who have strong intangible links, we co-designed a temporary exhibition highlighting our heritage research and outcomes from the Greater Lumbini Area with the Taiwanese Fo Guan Shan Buddha Museum between May and September 2018. Targeted at educating potential Buddhist pilgrims in their homeland before they travel, we attracted almost one million visitors. Over 2000 visitors responded to our survey, of whom 70% stated that the exhibition had given them a greater awareness of the heritage at risk at Buddhist pilgrimage sites in the Greater Lumbini Area. We also include practitioners and managers within our definitions of 'community' and, with funding from UNESCO, the Governments of Nepal and Sri Lanka, AHRC-GCRF, the Oriental Cultural Heritage Sites Protection Alliance and the British Council (India) and UK-India Education Resource Initiative, have facilitated exchange programmes for 100 archaeological and heritage officers. These participants were trained alongside 453 national staff and students in field techniques and interpretations and introduced to the research tools for managing sub-surface remains. A further 158 officers were introduced and trained in responding to heritage threats in post-disaster or post-conflict scenarios. For the latter, we ran field laboratories on-site at Jaffna Fort, where 91% of the 22 surveyed participants stated that they were better equipped to protect heritage after a disaster as a result of the training. Notwithstanding these clear engagement and impact successes, we conclude by stressing that our cascade is not a product but a process and we are already reviewing feedback and anticipate enhancing it in the future.

REFERENCES

Brown, J., & Hay-Edie, T. (2014). *Engaging Local Communities in Stewardship of World Heritage: A Methodology Based on the COMPACT Experience* (World Heritage Papers No. 40). Paris: UNESCO.

Coningham, R. A. E., Acharya, K. P., Davis, C. E., Weise, K., Kunwar, R. B., & Simpson, I. A. (2018). Look Down, Not Up: Protecting the Post-disaster Subsurface Heritage of the Kathmandu Valley's UNESCO World Heritage Site. In L. A. Bracken, H. Ruszczyk, & T. Robinson (Eds.), *Evolving Narratives of Hazard and Risk: The Gorkha Earthquake, Nepal, 2015* (pp. 159–181). London: Palgrave.

Molesworth, K., & Müller-Böker, U. (2005). The Local Impact of Under-Realisation of the Lumbini Master Plan: A Field Report. *Contributions to Nepalese Studies, 32*(2), 183–211.

Weise, K. (Ed.). (2013). *The Sacred Garden of Lumbini: Perceptions of Buddha's Birthplace*. Kathmandu: UNESCO.

INDEX

The manufacturer's authorised representative in the EU is Springer
Nature Customer Service Centre GmbH, Europaplatz 3, 69115 Heidelberg,
Germany. If you have any concerns regarding our products, please
contact ProductSafety@springernature.com

Printed and bound by CPI Group (UK) Ltd, Croydon, CR0 4YY
29/04/2026
02099478-0001